The Australian Geographic Book of

Lord Howe Island

Text and photography by Ian Hutton

GRAHAME McCONNELL

First published 1998
Reprinted 1999; reprinted with revisions 2003
by Australian Geographic Pty Ltd
PO Box 321, Terrey Hills NSW 2084, Australia
Phone: (02) 9473 6777, fax (02) 9473 6701
email: books@ausgeo.com.au
© Australian Geographic Pty Ltd 1998

Managing Director: Rory Scott
Managing Editor, Books: Averil Moffat

Editor: Ken Eastwood
Commissioning Editor: Ian Connellan
Design and Photographic Edit: John Witzig
Director of Cartography: Will Pringle
Print Production: Tony Gordon
Production Manager: Valerie Reed
Picture Research: Jacqueline Watson
Cartographer: Yvette Gnauck
Editorial Assistant: Susan McCreery

Text © Ian Hutton and Australian Geographic.
Photography © Ian Hutton unless otherwise credited.
Illustrations of palms, pandanus, Pacific black duck, buff-
banded rail, purple swamphen, masked lapwing and cattle
egret by Margaret Murray. All other bird illustrations by
Terrence Lindsey; all other plant illustrations by Ian Hutton.

Printed in Hong Kong by Dai Nippon Printing

Acknowledgements
For their assistance with this book, Australian Geographic
and Ian Hutton thank: Greg Leaman, Dean Hiscox, LHI Board;
Dr Alex Ritchie; Dr David Roots, Australian Academic Tours;
Des Griffin, Australian Museum; Dr Peter Fullagar; Tony
Whitaker; Peter Harrison, Southern Cross University; Barry
Conn, Royal Botanic Gardens, Sydney; and Jeff Deacon, Jack
Shick, Gower Wilson and other islanders who shared their
knowledge freely. Ian Hutton also thanks Chris Murray for his
support with the book over many years.

National Library of Australia Cataloguing-in-Publication Data:

Hutton, Ian, 1950-.
  The Australian Geographic book of Lord Howe Island.

  Bibliography.
  Includes index.
  ISBN 1 876276 27 4.

  1. Lord Howe Island – Guidebooks. 2. Lord Howe Island –
  History. 3. Lord Howe Island – Description and travel. I.
  Title.

919.481

Cover: *Framed by Mt Eliza's pointed summit and the southern mountains, Lord Howe's turquoise lagoon beckons.*

Back cover: *Just kicking back: island visitor Barry Hatton, in The Lagoon. Photo: Grahame McConnell.*

Title page: *Sooty terns wheel over Roach Island, 2 km north-east of Lord Howe.*

Pages 2–3: *The island's 1455 ha of beauty inspires all who have approached it by air, including 1950s visitors, who lumbered in by flying-boat.*

Pages 4–5: *Enjoying quiet sunsets on the jetty or fishing with friends: visitors have enjoyed Lord Howe's treasure-rich waters for decades.*

Page 6: *Clinging to the hillside on the climb to Goat House Cave, perched 400 m up Mt Lidgbird.*

Page 7: *Lord Howe's pied piper of fish, Brian Simpson, observed by visitors and a shark, at left, during his daily fish-feeding ritual.*

This page: *Kentia palm frond (above left); brain coral (above right).*

Opposite: *Toasting the occasion, wedding guests at PINETREES boat-shed celebrate with champagne and seafood.*

Contents pages: *Delightful and distinctive: Lord Howe's kentia palm forest.*

Contents

GRAHAME McCONNELL

Lord Howe Island is so extraordinary it is almost unbelievable. You can get to it within two hours from great cities. Yet, once there, you can see five species of bird and over 50 plant species that live nowhere else on earth. You can climb one of Lord Howe's peaks, clap your hands and shout and, at the right time of year, seabirds by the dozen will drop through the forest canopy and land trustingly at your feet. From its beaches you can wade out and swim over the most southerly large coral reef on the planet. And there is so little traffic that most visitors either cycle or walk everywhere. Few islands, surely, can be so accessible, so remarkable, yet so unspoilt.

Anyone with an eye for natural beauty could easily spend idyllic days on this magical island. Many of us, however, will want to seek out its special treasures. One, paradoxically, you may recognise almost immediately – for although Lord Howe is its original home, it can be seen in all parts of

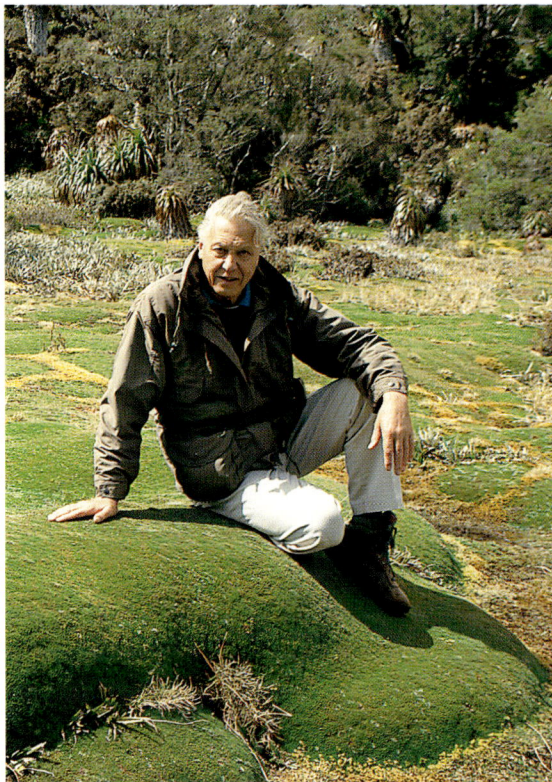

NEIL NIGHTINGALE/BBC NATURAL HISTORY UNIT

In 1998, Sir David Attenborough (above) – pictured near Mt Anne, Tasmania, on one of his many excursions to Australia – visited Lord Howe Island to film sequences for a documentary on birds. The island and its nearby islets are major breeding areas for many species, such as the masked booby (opposite). The largest bird to breed on LHI, with a wingspan of up to 170 cm, this booby species can be seen all year round.

the world. It is one of the hardiest and most decorative of all house plants – the Lord Howe kentia or thatch palm. But many of the other plants – pandanus and tree-ferns, orchids and asters – you are not likely to know for they grow nowhere else. You'll want to keep an eye out too for the island's special birds, one of which, the Lord Howe rail or woodhen, is still one of the rarest species in the world.

This book will enable you to enjoy all these things. And it does more. It explains how the island came to be raised above the surface of the ocean and tells you the fascinating story of the island's discovery and settlement. In short, the pages that follow will enable you to discover just how truly extraordinary Lord Howe Island really is.

David Attenborough

Lord Howe Island

Paradise on our doorstep, breathtakingly beautiful Lord Howe Island has been settled for 150 years but remains largely unspoilt. About 75 per cent of the island and its islets are preserved as permanent park. With a diversity of birds, many rare native plants, the world's southernmost coral reef, a brilliant blue lagoon and white, sandy beaches lined with palms, Lord Howe is a jewel on the World Heritage list. It's a popular tourist destination that is never crowded, for an official policy of restricting visitor numbers ensures its tranquil atmosphere.

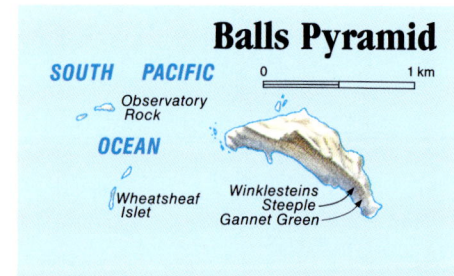

Admiralty
Tenth of June I.
Roach Island
Noddy Island   South Island
Islands   Sugarloaf I.
Sugarloaf Passage
Soldiers Cap   *Mokambo Rock*
Kims Lookout   *Malabar Hill 208*
North East Roadstead
Curio Point / Old Gulch
Fishy Point
Mount Eliza 147
New Gulch
Neds Beach
Catalina wreckage ×
Phillip Rock ∗ (awash)
Searles Point
Hells Gates
Stevens Point
Jims Point
North Head
North Bay
Dawsons Point
Old Settlement Beach
Hunter Bay
PO
Middle Beach   Valley of the Shadows
Jetty
Signal Point
North Passage
The Lagoon
Lagoon Beach
Clear Place Point
The Clear Place
Administration Office
Little Mutton Bird Ground
Blackburn Island
+ Transit Hill
LAGOON
Blinky Point
Blinky Beach
ROAD
Blackburn Island Passage
Sail Rock   **Mutton Bird I.**
Comets Hole
Airport   **Blinkenthorpe Bay**
Prince William Henry Bay
Cobbys Corner
Golf course
Mutton Bird Point
Lovers Bay
Intermediate Hill + 250
Erscotts Hole
Rocky Point
Kings Beach
Rocky Run
Erscotts Passage
Boat Harbour
Boat Harbour Point
Man of War Passage (South Passage)
Blind Passage
Salmon Beach
Goat House Cave
SOUTH   PACIFIC
East Point
Cut Grass Point
Far Flats
George Bay
Sugarloaf Point
South West Roadstead
Mount Lidgbird + 777
Little Island
Red Point
OCEAN
Erskine Valley
Worlds End
The Little Slope
Mount Gower + 875
The Big Slope
The Potato Hills
∗ George Rock (submerged)
South Head
King Point
Gower Island

N

∗ *Wolf Rock*

0 ___ 2 km

Balls Pyramid

SOUTH   PACIFIC
Observatory Rock
OCEAN
Wheatsheaf Islet
Winklesteins
Steeple
Gannet Green
0 ___ 1 km

Introduction

Over the past two decades I've made many treks to the summit of Lord Howe's highest peak, the awesome 875-metre Mt Gower. On one trip in the mid-1980s I was accompanied by Judy Lacey – the wife of one of Lord Howe's then administrators and a keen world traveller. With providence petrels swooping overhead, we gazed over the lush mist forest on the summit to a turquoise and blue patchwork of reef, lagoon and ocean. Echoing the opinions of residents and visitors alike, Judy said: "If you sat down with pen and paper to consciously design the perfect island, you could hardly improve on Lord Howe."

I couldn't agree more. Lord Howe Island (LHI) is stunningly beautiful, it's in a remote location and abounds in natural wonders – coral reefs with a diversity of life forms, teeming seabird colonies, rare land birds, diverse forest landscapes populated by indigenous plants, and a fascinating coastal terrain that includes steep cliffs, white sandy beaches and rock platforms latticed by tide pools. All this on a 1455-hectare scrap of land in the Tasman Sea, 770 kilometres north-east of Sydney.

We read about such unspoilt places, and often see them on television, but as time passes they become harder to find or overrun by hordes of visitors. Thanks to its 1982 World Heritage listing and years of careful planning for residential and tourist development, Lord Howe remains one of the world's few relatively untouched places: a domain where nature appears dominant and humans benignly coexist with plants and animals. No more than 393 tourists are allowed on the island at a time. You can walk or cycle everywhere and enjoy clean air and beaches, with nature always at your back door.

Glowingly described as "perpetual spring", the island's climate stays pleasantly mild throughout the year with only small daily and seasonal ranges in temperature. Summer maximums average 25°C and those of winter 18°C, with minimums a mild 19°C and 13°C respectively. These moderate temperatures, together with an absence of frosts and constant high humidity, promote the growth of Lord Howe's extensive subtropical rainforest. Precipitation mainly occurs as moderate to heavy showers rather than continuous rain, with about 180 millimetres falling in both June and July, dropping to a monthly 120 mm in summer.

Away from the small settled portion of LHI there's another world to explore – one of precipitous mountains bounded by rugged rocky coastline (above), their sheer windblown sides laced with rare, gnarled plants barely clinging on; and in stormy weather, gushing short-lived waterfalls like Dinner Run falls (opposite right). Two lifelong islanders, Ray Shick and Gower Wilson (opposite left), have a love of LHI that has seen them star in documentaries about their home. Gower, clutching a pig's curved tusk – a reminder of a time when the pair hunted feral pigs in Lord Howe's forests – even spends his annual holidays on the island. "Why would I go anywhere else?" he asks. "Everything I want is here."

Settled for more than 150 years, Lord Howe is relatively unspoilt, unlike many other remote islands. About 70 per cent of the island remains uncleared, despite settlers' heavy dependence on its resources, such as the valuable kentia palms. Today the 330-odd residents dote on their idyllic lifestyle: an existence that may include farming or fishing, collecting kentia seeds and servicing guests.

Although we can't all live there (it wouldn't be paradise then!), Lord Howe is within easy reach – only a two-hour flight from Sydney or Brisbane. But thankfully, the tourist industry has from its beginnings been based on the island's natural assets and this has been a major factor in LHI's preservation.

I hadn't heard of Lord Howe until 1980. I was 30 years old and a Bureau of Meteorology posting came up at the island's meteorological station, then at the north end of Middle Beach. I found an Australian Museum booklet on the place, and a little reading gave me visions of clambering around rainforest-clad mountains investigating plants and climbing tussocky cliffs to photograph seabirds. I'd no idea how much of my life Lord Howe would consume. The island inspired me so much that it became both a privilege and a duty to spend many years there studying nature and explaining its amazing diversity to others. Along the way I learned an enormous amount from other interested people – locals, tourists and visiting scientists.

My original two-year posting extended to four years. After a two-year break I returned, keenly looking forward to another four-year term. The job involved

shift work, which often meant starting at 2.30 a.m. – but early shifts meant early finishes, so I was often free to continue my explorations by 11 a.m.

During my years on Lord Howe I came to realise that a lot of scientific research had been completed on the island's 300-plus plant species, 166 different birds, nearly 500 fish species and many other animals, but most of the findings were inaccessible to the general public. I became fascinated by the information and, as a way to use my photographs and research notes, produced three books and a range of interpretive material for lay readers. After moving back to mainland Australia and resigning from the Bureau, I regularly returned to my mecca in the Pacific, taking small groups on personalised nature tours.

This book is the sum of more than eight years spent living on LHI, nearly two decades of research and innumerable interpretive tours. It's designed to be a field guide, reference book and souvenir of a very special place. Through the text, photographs, maps and drawings you'll see how the island was formed and how the sea, streams and land were populated by a host of life forms. You'll be introduced to many of the plants and animals – each with special adaptations that help them survive in an island environment. And you'll discover Lord Howe's fascinating human history, and the best ways to explore the island today.

It's my hope that *The Australian Geographic Book of Lord Howe Island* will contribute to a deeper understanding and enjoyment of LHI and its abundant treasures, by all those who venture – or dream of venturing – to its shores. Lord Howe has been good to me, and I trust that this book will reinforce in readers' minds the island's irreplaceable value.

Ian Hutton

Paradise born

Like a giant Gothic spire thrusting from a vast steel-blue pond, Balls Pyramid rears 551 m above the Tasman Sea. The basalt stack is a slender remnant of a former island – once 10 km in diameter – that was part of the same volcano responsible for the formation of LHI, in the distance. The aftermath of more than 100 lava flows can still be identified on it.

Fly across hundreds of kilometres of open ocean into sight of Lord Howe Island and you'll undoubtedly marvel at this magnificent, volcanic outcrop. The remote island's lush vegetation, sparkling lagoon and sandy beaches may belie its fascinating origins, but the rugged mountains in the north and south provide many clues to its fiery creation and erosion-shaped history. A journey deep beneath the sea would produce an even more detailed picture.

LHI and Balls Pyramid – a fantastic 551 m high spire, 23 km south-east of Lord Howe – are peaks of the same large underwater mountain that rises from the seabed 2000 m down. This mountain sits on the western edge of an undersea plateau known as the Lord Howe Rise. About 2000 km long by 300 wide, the rise extends from New Zealand to LHI, then north to Chesterfield Islands, midway between New Caledonia and the Queensland coast. Movements of the Earth's crust separated this rise from the Australian mainland about 80 million years ago (mya).

The western edge of the rise is bounded by a chain of flat-topped undersea mountains called guyots. The Lord Howe and Balls Pyramid guyot is the only one forming an island today, although the two closest – Middleton and Elizabeth reefs, more than 200 km north of LHI – are exposed at low tide. The guyots were submarine volcanoes that erupted in turn when the plate they're on moved north over a stationary "hot spot". Those to the north, being older and exposed to erosion and subsidence for a longer period, have disappeared from view. Above the surface, ongoing erosion is very fast and has had a dramatic effect. According to Sydney geologist Robert Coenraads, the sea will eventually cover Lord Howe.

"For all of its wonderful forests and ecosystems, the whole island will be awash within 200,000 years; a mere drop in the bucket when speaking of geological time. The island is almost entirely gone already – 97.5 per cent gone to be precise."

Lord Howe's northern hills provide perhaps the most startling evidence of these inexorable forces. Remnants of the volcanic eruptions that formed the bulk of the island 6.9 mya, these hills are now up to 700 m lower than they were when formed. At that time LHI was a gently sloping volcano known as a shield volcano and an area some 30 km in diameter stood above water.

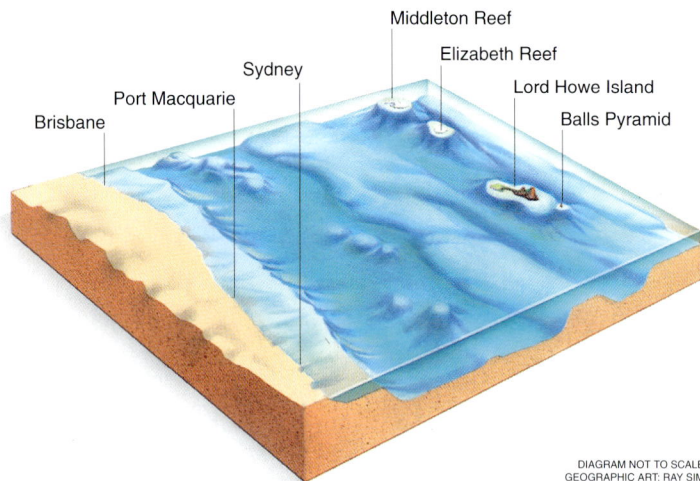

DIAGRAM NOT TO SCALE
GEOGRAPHIC ART: RAY SIM

Brisbane
Port Macquarie
Sydney
Middleton Reef
Elizabeth Reef
Lord Howe Island
Balls Pyramid

Lord Howe and Balls Pyramid are the most southerly in a chain of nine underwater volcanoes that stretches north for 1000 km. To the west, in the Tasman Basin, lies a parallel line of similarly eroded volcanic seamounts (above). The closest links in the Lord Howe chain, Elizabeth and Middleton reefs, were once islands, but now the eroded stumps capped by coral atolls are exposed only at low tide. Evidence of Lord Howe's volcanic origins is found in many dramatic island features, such as Hells Gates (above right), where volcanic ash consolidated into porous rock called tuff, which has been subsequently oxidised bright red. The dominating, erosion-resistant ramparts of 875 m Mt Gower and 777 m Mt Lidgbird (opposite) were formed about 6.4 million years ago as lava flows filled in the crater of the Lord Howe volcano.

The much higher southern mountains were formed more recently, about 6.4 mya. Geologists believe that the original volcano's summit collapsed, forming a crater about 5 by 2 km and 900 m deep. This final volcanic activity filled the crater with flat, thick layers of molten basalt, and the resistance of the layers resulted in the erosional remnants that are mounts Gower and Lidgbird. Visitors to Lord Howe can see evidence of basalt flows in several areas, but the best example is Mt Lidgbird's western cliffs. The finely textured flows are uniformly black and vary in thickness from a few centimetres to 30 m.

Two other volcanic rocks can be found on LHI: reddish tuff, which is made up of volcanic ash – fine dust that was expelled from the volcano and consolidated as it settled; and breccia, a fused mixture of red ash and black, angular blocks thrown from the volcano during an explosive eruption.

Features called dykes also remind visitors of LHI's volcanic past. These narrow seams of basalt were formed when molten magma was forced into cracks in the older rock. They're clearly visible at the southern end of Blinky Beach, Mutton Bird Point and Roach Island, 2 km north of Neds Beach. Hard and resistant to weathering, basalt dykes have formed many spurs in the northern hills, such as those leading to Malabar Hill and Mt Eliza. At Old Gulch, to the east of Mt Eliza, visitors have easy access to a range of volcanic features such as lava flows, breccias, dykes and ash beds. From Old Gulch it's also easy to see a large number of volcanic layers in Mt Eliza's eastern side.

The low-lying, central part of LHI is covered mainly by a white sedimentary rock called calcarenite. The grains of sand that make up this rock came from the skeletal

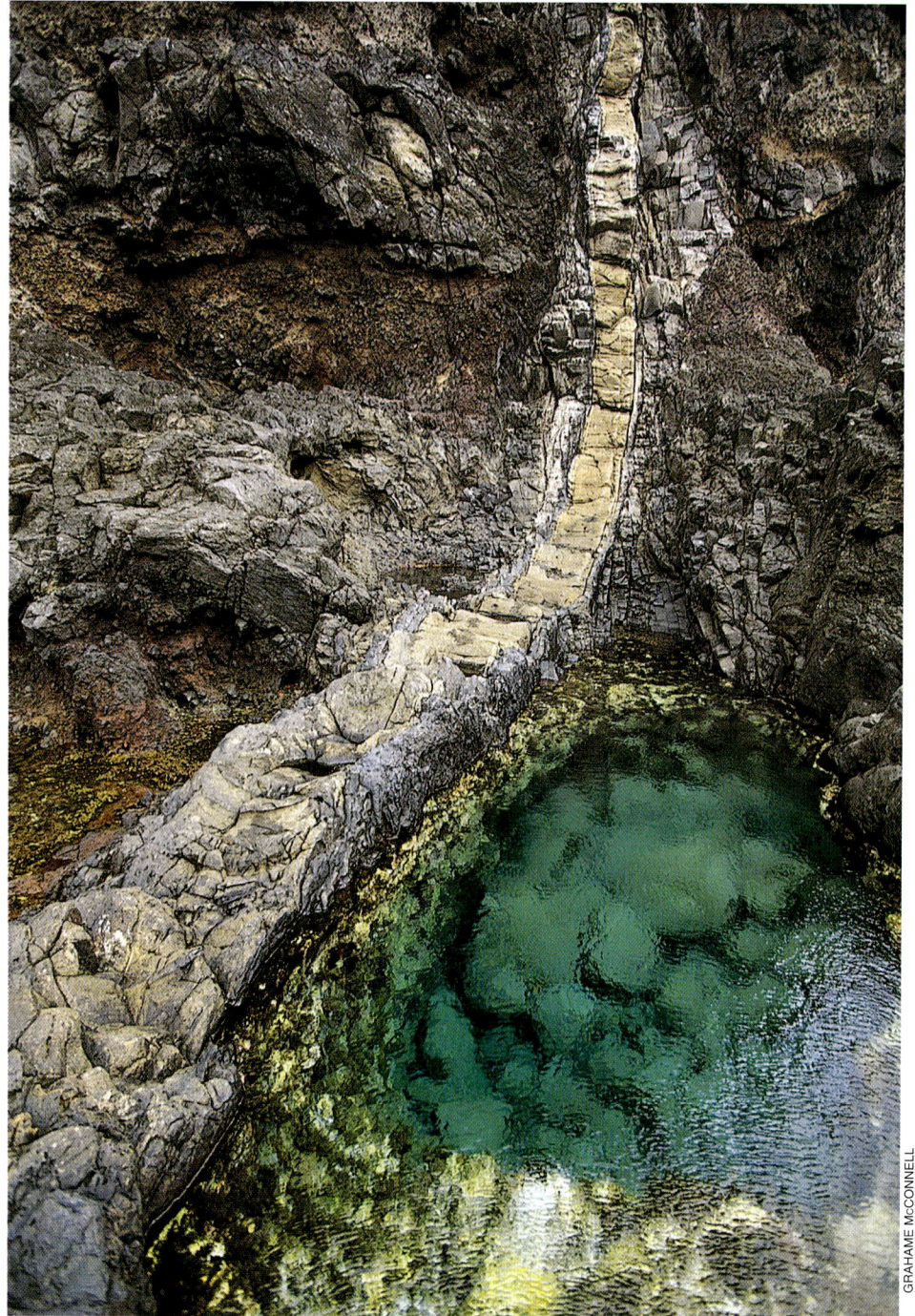

Spectacular near-vertical structures known as dykes stand out from the surrounding basalt rock at Mutton Bird Point (above) and Herring Pools (right). Visitors walk along the top of the 60 cm wide dyke at Herring Pools, marvelling that it was formed more than 6 million years ago, when cracks in the Lord Howe volcano were filled by molten lava. Dykes are highly resistant to weathering, and have formed spurs and ridges across the island, most obviously in the northern hills.

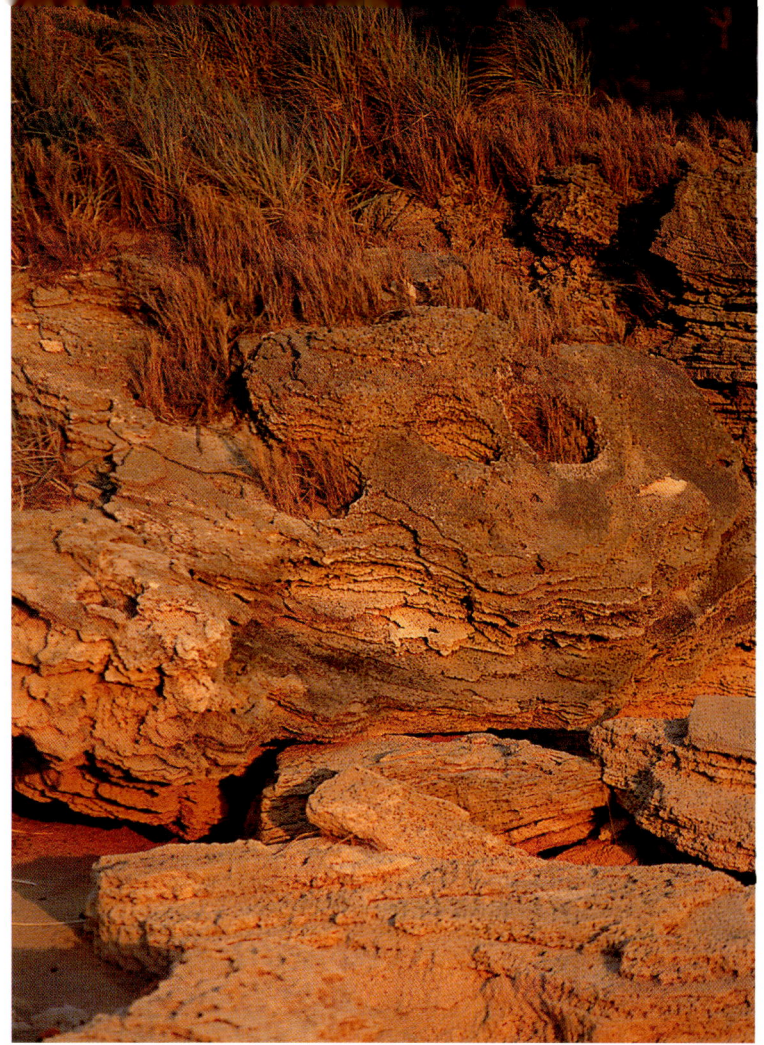

remains of billions of marine plants and animals that lived on the extensive wave-cut platform surrounding the island. As these organisms died, their fragmented remains were blown onto the island, gradually forming beaches and dunes. Judging by the widespread occurrence of calcarenite, the dunes were extensive during the last ice age – the sandy rock is found up to about 80 m on Transit Hill and the northern hills. Over time, rain soaking through the sand cemented the loose grains into a soft rock. Fossils in the calcarenite have been dated at 40,000–20,000 years, but it's believed that the calcarenite deposits at Neds Beach were formed around 130,000 years ago, when sea levels were roughly the same as today's.

On these ancient beaches, the Lord Howe horned turtle laid its eggs to incubate in the warm sand. At least 10 turtle skulls and hundreds of turtle bones and eggs have been found as fossils at and near Neds Beach and Old Settlement Beach. One of a group of extinct turtles with a horned skull and a long tail bearing bony rings, the Lord Howe turtle was a land dweller and probably lived behind the beaches, eating grasses and herbs. Similar fossils have been found in other southern hemisphere localities – in New Caledonia, mainland Australia and Argentina – indicating that the turtle's ancestors may have lived in Gondwana about 100 mya, before the southern supercontinent split up.

Many other fossils have been found in the calcarenite, including bird bones, eggs, and marine and land snails – wonderfully preserved reminders of a time when Lord Howe's range of plants and animals was quite different from today's.

Crumbly calcarenite (above) covers a large portion of the LHI lowlands. It consists of coral and shell debris that was blown onto the island, forming layered dunes up to 80 m above sea level in some places. Millimetre-thick horizontal layers in the sedimentary rock indicate the angle at which the material was deposited. Rich in calcium carbonate, the dunes were cemented together when rain soaked through the sand, forming a sedimentary rock. Tens of thousands of years later, erosion is breaking the grains apart. In the northern hills, groundwater saturated with the calcium carbonate trickled through cracks in small caves, forming decorative stalactites (above left) as it evaporated.

ANCIENT TURTLE FOUND IN POOL

In 1971, during excavation work for Ocean View Apartments' swimming pool, workers made a remarkable find – a well-preserved horned turtle skeleton. After the precious discovery was jackhammered out of the rock, part of the fossil was sent to the Australian Museum in Sydney. Ten years later it provided the basis for a skeleton reconstruction by the American Museum of Natural History, under the supervision of Dr Eugene Gaffney, the world's leading authority on horned turtles. One of four replicas cast in plastic and resin is displayed at the Lord Howe Island Museum.

Lighting up the imagination of local children (above right), a skeletal replica of the giant horned turtle MEIOLANIA PLATYCEPS, displayed in the LHI museum, is especially helpful when it comes to completing school projects. Sedimentary rocks on LHI have yielded a host of fossil remains, including former resident birds and the long-extinct turtle (above). Fossil fragments are still found today (below right) as the elements erode calcarenite around the coast.

EUGENE GAFFNEY

GRAHAME McCONNELL

Subject to the powerful, erosive forces of nature, Lord Howe is slowly disappearing. Today only about 2.5 per cent of the 7-million-year-old island remains. Once soaring 900 m above sea level, the northern hills are now a series of low peaks just 200 m high.

Life gains a foothold

Illustrating in lush hues the capacity for plants to colonise distant shores, virtually every trunk, rock and patch of ground on the summit of Mt Gower is now covered in greenery. Palms compete with tall rainforest trees; filmy ferns and mosses cover everything. Many people find it hard to believe that about 6 million years ago the same island summit was a glowing lava lake, surrounded by barren, hardened lava.

Once the lava that was eventually to become Lord Howe cooled, the long process of colonisation by plants and animals could begin – a process that culminated in the diverse natural environment we see today. It's the complexity and uniqueness of this environment that led to the Lord Howe Island group's World Heritage listing. The nomination document specifically mentions the group's exceptional natural beauty; diversity of landscapes, plants and animals; and the high proportion of rare and endemic (those restricted to an area) species.

The speed with which colonisation can occur on new volcanic islands has surprised scientists who have studied the process. Lord Howe's colonisation may also have been hastened by the last major ice age, which ended 20,000–10,000 years ago. So much water was locked up in ice that sea levels were as much as 100 m lower than they are today. Consequently, there were many more islands in the South Pacific Ocean that may have been used by animals and plants as migratory stepping stones. With a few exceptions, all of the island's plants, birds, reptiles and insects are either present, or have close relatives, on the nearest land masses – the Australian mainland, New Caledonia, New Zealand, Norfolk Island and, to a lesser extent, the more distant Pacific Islands.

Something in the air

The first animals to colonise the island were probably tiny scavenging insects that fed on decaying seaweed, fish and other marine animals washed onto the bare rock, but the first plants – mosses, lichens and ferns – dropped in by air. Their talcum-like spores were transported hundreds of kilometres by air currents until Lord Howe's mountains forced the moist, spore-bearing air to rise to cooler heights, causing the spores to fall to the ground in raindrops.

Breaking down the rock with their roots, these early arrivals helped build soil and their decaying remains added humus. Insects and earthworms, whose eggs may have arrived on the legs of visiting birds, also helped improve the soil's structure. Birds added guano, increasing the soil's fertility and helping larger plants, and eventually animals, to become established.

Some of the island's flowering plants have tiny seeds that could have been transported long distances by wind: they include orchids,

and trees such as the mountain rose, pumpkin tree and tea-tree. Other LHI plants have larger seeds with more food reserves to help them become established, and some of these – like the climbers *Parsonsia howeana* and *Clematis glycinoides* – use a parachute of silky hairs to float long distances through the air. About 10 per cent of the island's plant species probably arrived on air currents.

The main vertebrate (backboned) animals on Lord Howe are birds capable of flying long distances, and the island's only surviving bat species, the large forest bat, is also able to fly a long way. But some fliers not suited to long journeys are also found on Lord Howe. The eastern or purple swamphen – a rather ungainly flier – has been recorded as an irregular visitor for 200 years, and now breeds on the island. Small birds like the blackbird and song thrush flew to LHI in the 1940s, probably pushed by strong winds from New Zealand.

Riding the waves

If you walk along one of Lord Howe's beaches you'll find many seeds, some from plants already established on the island and others from distant shores, such as those of the box fruit and matchbox bean. About 17 per cent of the island's plants produce seeds that can float hundreds of kilometres from one shore to another. These seeds have a coat that prevents salt water penetrating and destroying the embryo inside. Plants producing such seeds usually grow along the seashore or on

Clinging to Mt Lidgbird's side, the yellow-flowering bush orchid (above) demonstrates how some plants vigorously establish themselves in seemingly sterile habitats. An endemic subspecies, the clumping plant has evolved from orchids that probably gained a foothold after their tiny seeds were transported hundreds of kilometres by wind. Ferns and mosses (right) would have arrived the same way, their countless tiny spores – as fine as talcum powder – lifted and carried by the slightest air currents. But crossing the ocean is only part of the colonisation process; to germinate and grow, a seed or spore must land where its moisture and nutrient requirements will be met.

Even after their seeds are thrown up by the sea on the hostile beach environment, some plants, such as IPOMOEA PES-CAPRAE (above left), germinate and flourish. Taking a different route to their new home, mosses produce capsules (above) of light spores that can be transported by wind, and silky hairs attached to the seeds of the vine MARSDENIA ROSTRATA (below right) and PARSONSIA HOWEANA (below left) form parachute-like structures that carry the seeds away.

riverbanks, from where the seeds can be swept into the ocean. Lord Howe has a smaller percentage of these plants than do most low-lying atolls because the island's beach areas, where the seeds are washed up, are relatively small.

Most such seeds fail to become established, but near the shore many plants with ocean-dispersed seeds have taken hold, such as the purple-flowering ground cover *Ipomoea pes-caprae* and the creeper *Canavalia rosea*. Further inland you'll come across burny bean, berrywood and beach lily.

The ancestors of Lord Howe's two lizard species may have arrived as adults or eggs travelling on whole trees or branches washed into the sea. Natural rafts like these can also transport seeds, non-flying insects and land snails.

Hitching a ride

About 40 per cent of the island's plants – including blackbutt, banyan and jasmine – produce fruits attractive to birds. After eating the enticing, colourful fruits, the birds deposit the hard seeds – which resist digestion – in droppings some distance from the parent plant.

Many of LHI's grasses and daisies produce small seeds with barbs, hooks or bristles that attach to fur and feathers. The punkwood tree has sticky seeds that adhere to feathers and may be transported considerable distances before being dislodged. The island's small snails and freshwater crab may have arrived as tiny eggs in mud stuck to the feet of migratory wading birds.

Visiting shorebirds are also thought to have played an important role in the island's colonisation. Many species will eat a range of plant foods on their travels and may deposit seeds with their droppings as well as carry them on their bodies.

Becoming established

Of the countless seeds, spores and tiny eggs that must have drifted, blown or been carried to LHI, relatively few survived, perishing unless they landed in a spot where conditions were suitable. Only about a quarter of the 166 bird species recorded at LHI have been able to establish permanent breeding populations. Butterflies have generally been more successful, but more than a third of the 24 recorded species have failed to establish breeding populations, probably owing to a lack of food for their caterpillars.

Unless a female arrives already pregnant, most animal species need at least a male and female to establish a population. Some plant species also need male and female individuals to reproduce. For many years a solitary pandanus or screw pine – a spreading tree of a species different from the other pandanus growing on the island – grew on the foreshore at North Bay. Although it flourished, growing to about 10 m, it never reproduced because it lacked a partner.

Another plant which appears to be unable to reproduce on the island is the burny bean, a vine growing vigorously near the shore at Boat Harbour, North Bay

GRAHAME McCONNELL

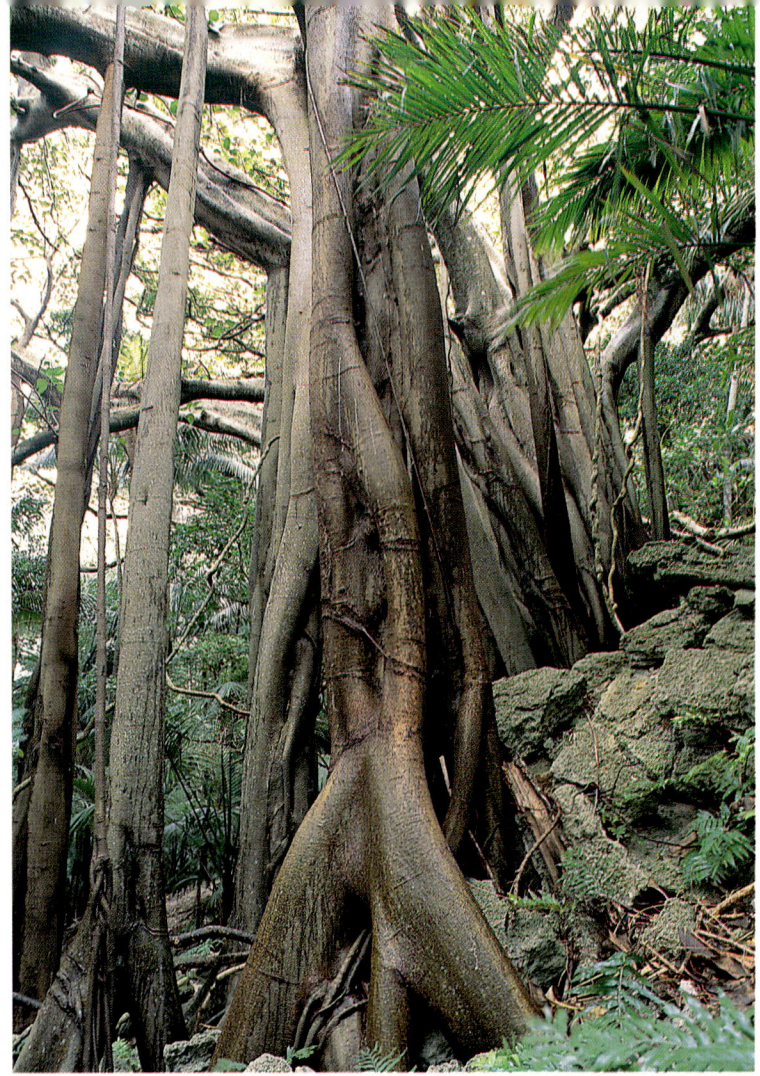

and Transit Hill. Its hairy fruit have never been seen on LHI, so it appears climatic conditions, or lack of a suitable pollinator, have prevented it from reproducing. But as long as the light, hard seeds keep arriving from distant shores and successfully germinate, the vine will retain a foothold on Lord Howe.

The island's natural environment is still changing. Since the Australian Museum's extensive environmental survey in the early 1970s, a fern, *Sticherus lobatus*, has begun growing on the summit of Mt Gower. In May 1987, a new species of helmet orchid was recorded by a visiting amateur botanist, possibly indicating it's a recent arrival. Several bird species have established breeding populations in recent times – welcome swallows in 1974, eastern swamphens in 1987 and masked lapwings in 1990.

Some of the island's plants and animals defy the usual colonisation conventions. For example, the island wedding lily has close relatives found only in southern

There is no doubt as to how the greybark (above left), banyan (above) and sweet-smelling jasmine vine (top left) reached Lord Howe. Their edible fruits enticed birds and the seeds, swallowed along with the fruits, were transported in the birds' stomachs and later ejected. Analysis of seeds shows that more of LHI's plants arrived on the island's windswept cliffs and rocky islets (opposite) in this way than by any other. Many plants disperse by producing seeds with barbs, hooks, bristles or sticky surfaces that attach to passing birds or other animals. Either way – inside or outside the carrier – seeds can be transported long distances from their parent plants.

Africa. Perhaps its buoyant corky seed managed to float the entire distance; or maybe it once existed on the Australian mainland, but has now become extinct there.

Another puzzling mystery is the former occurrence on the island of the extinct giant horned turtle. Over 1.5 m long, this land-dwelling reptile, whose feet weren't equipped for swimming, had relatives (now also extinct) on the Australian mainland, at Walpole Island near New Caledonia, and in Argentina. It's just possible that a male and female arrived simultaneously, floating on some type of natural raft – but this does stretch the imagination.

Adapting to their island home

Once Lord Howe was isolated by rising sea levels after the most recent ice age, plants and animals could adapt to their new environment with no further contribution from the "parent" species. Over time, large genetic changes resulted in plants and animals unique to the island. Thirteen of the 15 species of land birds recorded in 1788 are considered species or subspecies peculiar to the island, and about one-third of the native plants are unique, although related to plants elsewhere. Many invertebrates are also endemic.

Two flightless land birds, the woodhen and the now-extinct white gallinule, were among those recorded in 1788. With no predators to threaten them, these ground foragers had lost the ability to fly. This adaptation became a disadvantage once humans came on the scene.

Native blackbutt, a tree reaching 12 m high, is one of the island plants that shows the signs of adaptation to its environment. Growing under the dense rainforest canopy, young native blackbutts need to quickly grow large leaves to catch maximum light for photosynthesis, increasing their chance of survival. Mature trees therefore produce a black golf-ball-sized seed that provides plenty of stored nutrients for the new plant, helping it to grow rapidly. This large seed is too big for a bird to carry, nor does it have an impervious seed coat to permit dispersal on the open ocean. Yet, at one time the tree's ancestors almost certainly possessed one or both of these qualities, enabling it to reach Lord Howe.

Man-made changes to the environment have favoured some plant and animal species. Clearing for cattle grazing has benefited a few hardy island shrubs, such as the bully bush, which can compete against vigorous introduced grasses such as paspalum and kikuyu.

The sacred kingfisher and some other native birds may also have benefited from clearing as they prefer to hunt in open spaces. Two recent colonisers, welcome swallows and masked lapwings, probably couldn't have established themselves unless substantial clearing had taken place.

Humans arrived on LHI relatively recently and they have trod it fairly lightly. But it's clear their presence has altered the natural colonisation processes that have been at work since the island was formed.

GRAHAME McCONNELL

Among Lord Howe's commonly sighted birds are welcome swallows (opposite above left), masked lapwings (opposite below left) and eastern swamphens (opposite below right). They colonised Lord Howe relatively recently, once human changes to the environment – such as clearing for pasture (above) – made the habitat more suitable. Clearing also benefited sacred kingfishers (opposite above right) – striking birds that were present on the island when humans arrived – because it expanded the areas in which they forage for worms, beetles and other insects. They're often seen perched on fences looking for this prey, but are also found on rocky shores at low tide, feeding on small fish and crustaceans.

Human footprints

With the slow splash of oar strokes and islanders' farewells ringing in their ears, visitors are rowed from Neds Beach to the Burns Philp vessel SS MORINDA, which brought tourists to LHI from 1932 to 1939. As a long ocean voyage was the only means of getting to Lord Howe up to this time, the remote island was spared overdevelopment.

For millennia – while humans occupied and explored most other parts of the world – Lord Howe Island remained untouched. In fact, the island wasn't discovered by Europeans or Polynesians until 1788. Since then it's seen many changes as humans use, and endeavour to preserve, the island's rich natural resources.

Visitors to Lord Howe can view relics and photographs, and gain insight into the island's history at the LHI Historical Society Museum, a one-time Returned Services League memorial hall at the corner of Lagoon and Middle Beach roads. "I think Lord Howe is fascinating," says the museum secretary and island's airline agent Chris Murray. "It's got a history that goes back to the First Fleet and the way its sociology has developed is very interesting."

When the First Fleet sailed from England on 13 May 1787, Governor Arthur Phillip had orders to establish a primary settlement at Botany Bay, and a penal outpost at Norfolk Island, 2000 km to the north-east. HMS *Supply*, under the command of Lieutenant Henry Lidgbird Ball, was en route to Norfolk on 17 February 1788, when those aboard sighted an island. Ball named it Lord Howe's Island after the first lord of the British Admiralty, Richard Howe. During the return voyage to Sydney Cove, *Supply* anchored off the island's west coast on 13 March and a landing party went ashore to take possession in the name of the British Crown. The officers' diaries describe an abundance of large sea turtles and many birds that were caught and eaten. They particularly refer to the apparent tameness of the birds.

Government ships travelling between Sydney and Norfolk Island, until the latter's penal settlement was abandoned in 1814, often visited Howe's Island (as it was called), as did the mainly American whaling and trading vessels that pushed into the South Pacific. Some callers released goats and pigs on the island to provide fresh meat for later visitors.

No-one settled on LHI until 45 years after its discovery and there are few records to indicate what impact early visitors had. Although rugged terrain and thick vegetation probably limited the damage hunters could do, two species of land bird – the white-throated pigeon and the white gallinule – were hunted for food and probably became extinct even before the island was settled.

Lord Howe Island was named after Richard Howe (opposite above), Earl of Langor and first lord of the British Admiralty at the time of the island's discovery in 1788. It had no permanent residents until 1834, when a few settlers cleared a small area on the island's north-west. Today this area (opposite below) is known as Old Settlement. The population grew slowly; nearly 50 years later about half of the islanders gathered for a photograph (right) when Commissioner J. Bowie Wilson visited to investigate charges laid against island administrator Captain Richard Armstrong. Surviving mainly on what their immediate environment could provide, the 19th-century settlers took flesh-footed shearwater, or muttonbird, chicks for food (above) and built houses (above right) entirely from palm trees, using split trunks for frames and fronds for thatched walls and roofs.

Early settlement

Those who plied the Pacific Ocean for its rich stocks of whales in the early and mid-1800s often stopped at Polynesian, Melanesian and Micronesian islands to replenish their ships' stores. But further south, inhabited islands became fewer, providing opportunities for entrepreneurs to establish bases from which to supply passing ships.

With such an enterprise in mind, three Englishmen from New Zealand – Ashdown, Bishop and Chapman – moved with their families to LHI in 1834. They landed on the east coast at what is now called Blinky Beach and settled below the north hills, on the flat, easily farmed land behind Old Settlement Beach. As well as providing meat and vegetables to passing whaling ships, they collected feathers of the flesh-footed shearwater or muttonbird, which were shipped away in large quantities for stuffing pillows.

Seven years later the three men were bought out for £350 (about $30,000 today) by retired naval officer Captain Owen Poole and Richard Dawson, the owner of an important Sydney iron foundry. Later that year Poole imported several men and their wives to continue the industry started by Ashdown, Bishop and Chapman. One of the families, the Andrews, still has descendants living on the island today.

More settlers arrived in the following years and LHI was visited by up to 60 whaling and small trading vessels a year. "The island's very conscious of its maritime history," Chris says. "In the museum we've got a cannon that was probably traded by a schooner for supplies in 1880."

Several mariners returned to this peaceful, fertile backwater to settle, among them Nathan Thompson, who arrived about 1853. He and his wife Bogue raised two boys and three girls, and most of today's residents claim some connection to this family. Thompson brought the first horse to the island and built the first timber house from planks sawn from local trees and cedar logs washed onto the beach. It still stands where it was built, between Neds Beach and Signal Point.

Whaling declined dramatically in the 1870s and the islanders faced hard times as fewer and fewer vessels called at Lord Howe. From 1873 to 1876, no whaling ships at all are reported to have called. In 1876, Alfred Corrie, surgeon on the visiting HMS *Pearl*, noted: "now this once much frequented and favoured little spot is apparently, quite deserted; the old families have lost all zeal for cultivation, having to live, as it were, from hand to mouth, seeing the fruits of their labour decaying and rotting in the storehouses". The islanders knew that if their home was to prosper financially, they'd need a new industry.

REPRODUCTION OF MATHER BROWN'S PAINTING OF EARL HOWE

GRAHAME McCONNELL

Once illustrations of kentia palms (above) appeared in European plant catalogues in the early 1870s, demand soared and economic conditions for the islanders changed remarkably. In 1876, England's GARDENER'S CHRONICLE noted: "Among the hardier palms KENTIA FORSTERIANA deserves special mention, because it is so well adapted for cultivation in a cool house." The islanders' increasing dependence on this cash crop helped ensure the preservation of the dense lowland forest, thick with palms (opposite below). Ingenious harvesters quickly learnt to "shell" seeds from spikes by running them through a slot in a box lid (opposite above).

Kentia industry

From the early 19th century it became fashionable for wealthy Europeans to grow plants from faraway places. Plant groups that came into vogue included ferns, orchids, bromeliads (the group that includes pineapples) and palms.

Sydney Botanic Gardens director Charles Moore drew Europe's attention to the kentia or thatch palm after he visited Lord Howe in 1869, and by 1871 live plants were advertised for sale in European plant catalogues. Among the many palm species from the Pacific islands that found their way to Europe, kentias were particularly sought after. As the *Journal of Horticulture* reported in 1885: "These kentias are in greater demand than almost any other palm on account of their great beauty and enduring properties." Many Lord Howe residents recognised the palm's value as an export commodity and joined in the trade. As Chris says: "Economics of life here controlled everything. Islanders recognised the economic potential of palm seed. They all worked together and it brought a lot of prosperity to the island."

The island's first administrator, Captain Richard Armstrong, encouraged the export of palm seed, pandanus seed and palm fibre (which grows under the kentia's leafy crown). A retired Royal Navy officer, Armstrong had in 1878 been appointed administrator by the NSW Government, becoming LHI's forest ranger, postmaster, registrar of births, deaths and marriages, resident magistrate and clerk of petty sessions. An energetic man, he built the island's first road, Lagoon Road, introduced and experimented with many new crops, employed the first schoolteacher and cleared rock partially blocking the north passage into the lagoon. But some islanders, who may have seen his efforts to expand the seed-export business as a threat to their own enterprises, laid trumped-up charges against him, including one of supplying his stock of medicinal alcohol to locals. Armstrong was discharged from duty in 1882 by Commissioner J. Bowie Wilson, but two Parliamentary committees subsequently exonerated him and in 1885 he was awarded £3000 (about $160,000 today) in compensation.

The trade in palms and seed rapidly increased with nurserymen from Australia and Europe competing for supplies and with the introduction of a cash economy, the islanders' prosperity increased substantially. The simple thatched-palm cottages, typical up to the early 1880s, were replaced by modest timber-framed houses with iron roofs.

In the mid-1890s erratic visits by small coastal trading vessels gave way to a more regular steamship service operated by Burns Philp – an indication of the increased level of trade. But the trading boom wasn't all good news. Sometimes seed was exported but not paid for, with the excuse that it had been damaged and failed to germinate, so some residents tried to form a cooperative to maintain prices and protect their interests. In 1906 the Kentia Palm Seed and Plant Co. Ltd was formed and £1 ($43 today) shares were issued to 28 islanders, three mainland seed importers and Sydney agent Frank Farnell. Seed prices were fixed at the handsome rate of £2 a bushel (a bushel is about 36 litres, about the capacity of a washing basket). To help develop export opportunities, the Australian Palm Seed Export Co. Ltd was established in 1909, exporting 965 bushels in its first year and 1215 bushels in 1910.

These arrangements appeared to work well, but after a few years tensions arose between the mainland shareholders and the islanders, prompting the NSW Government to set up two Royal Commissions into the industry. Both concluded that the prosperity of the island was heavily dependent on the palm trade and the industry should be regulated by the Government for the benefit of the islanders. As Commissioner Walter Bevan wrote in 1912: "No other industry to be carried out on the island could possibly compete with the palm-seed industry. It would be suicidal to clear away the palms for the purpose of introducing other crops or plants, which can never be expected to return anything like the profit that this natural growth of the soil produces." A Board of Control was set up, consisting of three Government-appointed mainlanders, and a limited liability cooperative company was created in which all islanders were given shares.

PHOTOS: COURTESY HAZEL PAYTEN

RICHARD MORRIS/LHI HISTORICAL SOCIETY

The birth of tourism

With a route that included Sydney, Lord Howe and Norfolk islands and the New Hebrides (now Vanuatu), the Burns Philp steamships brought casual visitors to the island on a regular basis, forming the beginnings of a tourist trade. Passengers bound for other ports often preferred life ashore while their ships were loading and unloading, and island families began accommodating these visitors in their own homes. Before long, tourists were choosing the island as a holiday destination in its own right, staying at Lord Howe between ships. In the early 20th century the Andrews/Nichols family at Pinetrees and the Wilsons at Ocean View became the first to systematically cater for visitors. Before the outbreak of World War II there were about 60 guesthouse beds available.

By the mid-1930s, steamers called in at regular nine- and 19-day intervals and Pacific Island cruise ships came intermittently, ferrying passengers ashore for guided day-walks. This infant tourist industry was completely dependent on Lord Howe's natural beauty – no thought was given to the development of sophisticated shopping or entertainment facilities.

The Pacific Island routes of ships such as the 1800-ton SS Morinda (above) and its predecessors sparked a fledgling but important tourist industry. From the 1920s, the trading company Burns Philp promoted tourism in the Pacific as an adjunct to its cargo-handling and trade activities. Company publications described Lord Howe in glowing terms: "There are plenty of birds, but few animals, no snakes and no vermin … One could easily go into raptures over a climate that is like perpetual spring, where the temperature is never above 82 and never lower than 50 degrees [28–10°C]." Island residents took guests into their homes and separate accommodation was built, such as these small wooden huts at The Pines (right), near Windy Point. The site later became Pinetrees and now offers accommodation for up to 82 guests.

ROY BELL/COURTESY HAZEL PAYTEN

The war years

Although the establishment of the Board of Control was a major step in securing fair prices and orderly marketing for palm seeds, the industry suffered a number of setbacks. With the outbreak of WWI in 1914, the market for luxury items like indoor palms drastically declined. Seed was still harvested for the Australian market, but in much-reduced quantities.

The seed industry suffered a further setback in 1918, when the Burns Philp steamer *Makambo* struck a submerged rock off Neds Beach and had to be careened for repairs. Most of the cargo was removed from the vessel for safe storage, making it easy for rats to get onto the island. With no natural predators these pests quickly multiplied, eating not only palm seeds but the eggs and young of bird species, causing the extinction of five species within a decade. These birds had assisted in the control of weevils that damaged the flowers and seeds of the kentia palm and seed harvests declined considerably. In an effort to stop the rat plague, the Board of Control imported 80 owls and supplied light shotguns and ammunition to island residents, who were paid a bounty on rat tails – starting at 1 penny (about 10c today) per tail in 1920, and growing to sixpence (50c) a tail in 1928.

The world economic depression, which began in 1929, had only a minor impact on the industry because the kentia palm was a luxury item and many of the rich were not greatly affected by conditions at the time. In the 1930s the Board experimented with a small nursery on the island, aiming to export seedlings rather than seed. Declining demand later in the decade forced the Board to cut shareholders' payments and peg back the rat bounty to fourpence (about 40c now) a tail. Residents who were receiving income from the growing tourist industry were partly or wholly excluded from holding shares in the palm-seed industry.

With the outbreak of WWII in 1939, the palm and seed markets collapsed and the Board was forced to suspend shareholders' payments altogether. Most ships in the Burns Philp fleet were assigned to naval transport and support duties, so the frequency of the island's shipping service declined dramatically. Sailing schedules were unpredictable and, to minimise the ever-present danger of submarine attack, were not advertised.

Two large directional navigation and radio communication towers, built in 1938–39, can still be seen near the junction of Neds Beach and Anderson roads. During the war, a radio communications and meteorological station was manned 24 hours a day in a sandbagged building that now serves as the visitor centre. A coast-watch post was maintained on Malabar Ridge, and an emergency radio transmitter hidden on Transit Hill. Although Lord Howe survived WWII without close contact with the enemy, an anti-ship mine washed up on Middle Beach and had to be detonated. The RAAF maintained some surveillance of the area, but the only lifeline between Lord Howe and the mainland for urgent supplies, resident

Sadly, but perhaps inevitably with cargo ships servicing the island, rats made it ashore in 1918. They ate five bird species to extinction in less than a decade and devoured kentia seeds (above), drastically reducing the islanders' income. The only means of rat control at the time was shooting, and a bounty was paid on tails, which were often preserved in jars of methylated spirits (top) until payday.

At the fringes of cleared areas around the settlement, where dense forests give way to lush pastures, kentia and curly palms are slowly disappearing. Older trees are dying and the island's 100-odd head of beef and dairy cattle often destroy seedlings.

travel and the occasional medical evacuation was a once-a-month Catalina from the Rathmines Flying Boat Base on Lake Macquarie, about 100 km north of Sydney.

After the collapse of the seed-export and tourism industries, the Board recognised the need for urgent action and in 1940 arranged for a superintendent to take up residence to encourage self-sufficiency in food production, and to develop the commercial production of vegetable and flower seeds. This self-sufficiency drive led to the clearing of more native forest for grazing: on the lower slopes of Malabar Ridge above Old Settlement Beach and Middle Beach Common.

Postwar

Islanders had no real tenure over their residential land until the Commonwealth Government passed the *Lord Howe Island Act, 1953*. For the previous 119 years they'd virtually been squatters. In 1951, the Hon. Clive Evatt QC had recommended that 99-year leases be granted to residents. The island community was split over the proposal, as some believed the leases could easily be sold to outsiders. A few leases were issued, but the State Government withdrew them when the Lord Howe Island Act was passed. Under the Act, all land remained the property of the Crown, but direct descendants of those who had permissive occupancies in 1913 were given perpetual leases on blocks of up to 2 ha for residential purposes, and short-term special leases on larger tracts for pastoral and agricultural activities.

The Board was empowered to administer the new Act and the prewar Island Advisory Committee was retained to provide advice. The Act was amended in 1982 to give islanders a majority representation of three members on a five-man Board, and to extend islander status to those who had resided on the island for 10 years or more.

Palm-seed industry recovers

In the immediate postwar period, the palm-seed industry recovered slowly. Islanders were paid a bounty to collect the seed, and profits from sales were used for administration and to employ residents to carry out public works.

Demand for palm seed remained at around 300 bushels a year until the early 1960s, when Europeans again became eager to purchase seed. Overseas complaints about short supply resulted in additional seed being obtained from well-established trees on Norfolk Island and in Sydney. By the late 1970s, it was estimated that two-thirds of all kentia seed exported from Australia came from these sources.

The Board established its own nursery in the 1970s and by 1981 it was exporting only live seedlings. It's now the largest kentia nursery in the world, producing 3 million seedlings each year.

THE KING OF THE POTTED PALMS

Why, nearly 130 years after it was first described by scientists, is the kentia still one of the world's most popular indoor palms? The answer in part is that it evolved over millennia on Lord Howe, where average temperature, humidity and ambient light are much lower than in the tropics, where most palms occur naturally. As a result of this evolutionary conditioning, the kentia is quite at home indoors – especially in Europe – where tropical palms don't fare so well.

No less important is the kentia's distinctive visual appeal. "The palm is not only very hardy, it's graceful and decorative," says Dutch businessman Henk van Staalduinen, the biggest importer of kentias into Europe. "For indoors, there is no better palm. People have tried all over the world to find species to match the kentia, but fortunately for Lord Howe Island nobody has ever succeeded, and I'm sure that they never will."

Soaring to 15 m (above left), the kentias that give LHI its distinctive tropical appearance (left) are coveted as hardy and attractive house plants all over the world. In a Dutch hothouse (above), importer Henk van Staalduinen, at left, is dwarfed by rows of healthy specimens destined for European office complexes.

By the mid-1930s, with steamships arriving at regular nine- and 19-day intervals, island life was far from Spartan. Mountains of supplies were pushed and pulled up the jetty (above left), providing islanders with all the mainland comforts – the latest fashions, furnishings and even wirelesses (left). Fishing (above) continued to be a major source of food and recreation for residents and visitors, with nearly every trip producing a good catch of temperate and tropical fish, including kingfish, tuna and trevally. The most extensive fish survey in Lord Howe waters was undertaken in 1973. The month-long study, sponsored by the National Geographic Society, brought the total number of fish species recorded in island waters to 447, from 107 families. Nearly 50 species have since been added to this list.

The growth of tourism

In 1940, nine years after Englishman Francis Chichester landed his Gypsy Moth float plane *Madame Elijah* on LHI's lagoon – becoming the first to land a plane at the island – the Board of Control raised the possibility of a commercial air service to Lord Howe. "It is felt that the establishment of a flying-boat service between Sydney and Lord Howe Island would provide a facility that would contribute immeasurably to make Lord Howe Island one of the leading, if not the premier, tourist resort of Australia," the Board said in a memorandum to residents.

After WWII a number of entrepreneurial ex-airforce personnel became interested in commercial aviation. One airline employing such people – Trans Oceanic Airways – began a commercial flying-boat service to LHI, using converted Sunderlands, after responding to an urgent medical evacuation in 1947, during which the lagoon was found to be a suitable landing area. Later that year Qantas opened a service with Catalina flying boats, but competition on such a small route was unprofitable and Qantas withdrew in 1951. When Trans Oceanic Airways wound up in 1953, Ansett Airways took over the LHI service using Sandringhams until 1974, when a 900 m airstrip was built. The airstrip solved the problem of timing flights to coincide with high tides.

For the next 15 years, the island's tourism industry experienced moderate prosperity, with a succession of commuter airlines maintaining services from Sydney, Brisbane and Port Macquarie. All services operated planes that could carry a maximum of 10 passengers until 1990, when Norfolk Airlines leased a new 36-seater aircraft with short take-off and landing capabilities. Eastern Australia Airlines took over the Lord Howe–Sydney service in June 1991, and that company and Sunstate Airlines (both now subsidiaries of Qantas) continue to provide the backbone of the service.

To a remarkable extent, the nature of postwar aviation to Lord Howe has helped protect it from overdevelopment. Until 1974, the flying-boat services were unable to carry more than about 5000 visitors a year, and by the time larger aircraft arrived on the scene, environmental and planning safeguards had been put in place by the NSW and Federal governments, culminating in the island's World Heritage listing in 1982.

LHI HISTORICAL SOCIETY/COURTESY MABEL MORRIS

RICHARD MORRIS/LHI HISTORICAL SOCIETY

Flipped during the night by strong winds, Francis Chichester's Gypsy Moth MADAME ELIJAH *(above right) lies with its nose in Hunter Bay in March 1931. Chichester had safely arrived from Norfolk Island in the storm – becoming the first to fly to Lord Howe – despite a failed radio, compass and air-speed indicator. After two months making repairs, he completed his Tasman Sea crossing. From 1947 to 1974 British-built Sandringhams (right) regularly landed on the lagoon, ferrying visitors to and from Sydney.*

In the 1930s, with tourism increasingly becoming the island's major money-spinner, visitors had countless ways to enjoy LHI – from trips to North Bay in Pinetrees' launch ALBATROSS *(top), to quiet times in charming guesthouses like* OCEAN VIEW *(above). Tourists are enticed in much the same way today as in a 1930s* OCEAN VIEW *brochure: "Lord Howe Island with its wealth of mountains and tropical scenery, is ever calling ... a veritable artists' and photographers' Arcadia."*

ROMANCE OF AN ISLAND WEDDING

In recent years, Lord Howe has grown in popularity with Australian mainland couples as a venue for their weddings. From 1894 to 1980, only 16 marriages in which both partners were mainlanders were recorded on Lord Howe. From 1980 to 1997, this number increased dramatically to 95. Mainland couples who tied the knot island-style in 1998 included David Whittaker and Lisa Green (below), shown during their ceremony at Lovers Bay.

The island's first recorded wedding set the precedent for romantic escapism. In 1843, Alan Isaac Mosely, navigation officer on the whaler *Jane*, met and fell in love with his wife-to-be Johanna in Sydney. Obviously besotted, he smuggled her aboard in a large crate, but she was discovered by the ship's master after they'd put to sea. It was decided to set her ashore at the first landfall, which happened to be Lord Howe Island. When *Jane's* voyage was completed, Mosely returned to Lord Howe, where he and Johanna were married by Captain Poole. The couple remained island residents for the rest of their lives.

Snorkelling trips (right) are one of the more popular activities provided by island tour operators. The sheltered waters of the crystal-clear lagoon (above) provide safe and exhilarating snorkelling for novices and old hands alike, and amazing displays of corals and fish life are found a short boat ride from shore. More and more, visitors to this magical island are coming to see and appreciate its many natural wonders – a legacy of a long-standing tourism industry that has focused on the island itself, rather than garish, human-made "attractions".

PHOTOS: GRAHAME McCONNELL

EDGAR WAITE/COURTESY SA MUSEUM

Scientists have long taken a great interest in LHI. According to Sydney botanical consultant Tony Rodd, Lord Howe's distance from the mainland and other large islands makes it "one of the more fascinating places in the world for the study of island biography". Much of the research that has taken place wouldn't have been possible without the assistance of islanders, who often provided transport for expeditions, such as this one (above) to North Bay in 1904. Although not a trained scientist, zoological collector Roy Bell (opposite) made a great contribution to knowledge – particularly of island birdlife – during his 18-month sojourn on LHI in 1913–14. He spent many nights camping in the mountains in search of bird, snail and plant specimens, which were sent to museums around the world.

Studying the natural heritage

Lord Howe's extensive range of plants and wildlife has generated so much scientific interest that in the past century about 250 studies have been published on the island's animals and 100 on its plants. In many of these studies, islanders have played an important role: guiding scientists, helping parties get to remote areas such as Mt Gower and the offshore islets, and supplying local knowledge of plants and animals.

The first observations on the natural history of LHI were recorded by men on First Fleet ships dispatched to Norfolk Island. Artists George Raper and John Hunter painted some of the native birds, including the white gallinule and white-throated pigeon, leaving our only visual records of these animals.

In the early 19th century explorers from many nations traversed the Pacific Ocean and described many of the plants and animals on and around LHI. Between 1851 and 1854, the British survey ship HMS *Herald* charted island waters while naturalist William Milne collected plant specimens and sent them to the Royal Botanic Gardens at Kew, England, and John MacGillivray catalogued fishes and birds. He failed to find any woodhens, "their numbers having been thinned by the wild cats, the descendants of those landed by the master of a Sydney whaler five or six years ago".

In 1851 island resident Dr John Foulis was asked to supply a report to the colonial government, which was considering the establishment of a penal colony on Lord Howe. His report included brief notes on the island's plants and animals, its topography and geology. Fortunately, the idea of a penal colony was quietly dropped.

The information gathered on plants during the next 30 years enabled Ferdinand von Mueller to publish the first comprehensive list of island plants in 1875, describing 195 species. Seven years later a team of scientists from institutions including the Australian Museum and the Sydney Botanic Gardens accompanied Commissioner Wilson, setting up a long association between the island and these institutions. The Australian Museum played the leading role, sending its first official expedition to Lord Howe in 1887, leading to the classic 1889 natural history text *Memoirs No. 2*.

The greatest early contribution to the knowledge of island birdlife was made when London book publisher Gregory Mathews employed the zoological collector Roy Bell to visit Norfolk and Lord Howe islands in 1911–13. Bell was the first to record Kermadec petrel breeding at Lord Howe. His specimens were sent to London to assist Mathews in the preparation of the impressive 1928 publication *Birds of Norfolk and Lord Howe Islands*, which contains descriptions and coloured drawings of all LHI's breeding land birds and six species of seabirds.

Later researchers included the Australian Museum's H.J. de Disney, who throughout the 1970s spent weeks on the summit of Mt Gower, then the only

EDERIC SLATER

The woodhen, the subject of curiosity for some island lads in the 1920s (left), became the object of intense scientific study in the 1970s after it was realised the species was facing extinction. Researchers (above, left to right) John Disney, Alan Morris and Peter Fullagar spent weeks on Mt Gower's summit – then the woodhen's last remaining refuge – studying the bird's biology and ecology.

remaining habitat of the woodhen. A two-year study of the bird was carried out from 1978 by ornithologist Dr Ben Miller and his findings formed the basis of a program to rescue the endangered creature. After feral cats and pigs were removed from the island, captive-bred birds were released in areas where they'd not been recorded for more than a century. Now woodhens can be found all over the island.

When Peter Green, deputy director of Kew Gardens, visited the island in 1963, he was alarmed at the impact goats were having on vegetation and alerted government authorities to the damage being done. As a result, staff of the Australian Museum and the Sydney Royal Botanic Gardens began the most extensive environmental survey ever undertaken on LHI to assess all threats (including future development) to the island's environment. The resulting report, completed in 1973 and now known as the Recher report, has been a fundamental document in environmental planning. Its recommendations included the creation of reserves and control programs for introduced weeds and feral animals.

More than any other single factor, the extensive documentation of Lord Howe's unique natural history, and the recommendations of visiting scientists, gave the NSW Government, and ultimately the Federal Government, the incentive to protect the island.

Despite 150 years of predation by cats and habitat disturbance by feral pigs, woodhens show little fear, as Mt Gower guide Jack Shick (above) knows. The birds, now safely breeding on LHI thanks to a successful species-recovery program, can be seen in many parts of the lowlands, spreading their chestnut-and-black wings (left) in warm patches of sunlight that break through the canopy. Around 220 individuals now live on the 1455 ha island, and that's believed to be about the maximum viable population. Intensely territorial, woodhen pairs defend their domains of about 3 ha from potential invaders by calling loudly with a repeated high-pitched ringing call. This territorial cry is easily distinguished from the birds' normal low "bonk".

A coiled, fraying rope (opposite) reminds passers-by of Lord Howe's maritime history and isolation in the South Pacific – a position that has helped preserve so much of its beauty. Although early generations of islanders (below right) had some impact on Lord Howe's wilderness areas, the tyranny of distance dramatically restricted the number of visitors to the island, and about 70 per cent of it remains untouched, enabling current and future visitors to fully appreciate this World Heritage area. Today, visitor numbers at any one time are limited to a maximum of 393 so the atmosphere of a peaceful paradise pervades. Keen birdwatchers (below) are among those drawn to this unique environment – often as part of organised nature tours – observing and photographing the 18 land birds and 14 seabirds that breed on the island.

Preservation

From Armstrong's 1878 brief to "prevent the destruction and removal of indigenous trees, and to guard against the destruction of animals", to the 1953 Lord Howe Island Act, which states that the Board shall "take all practical measures to protect and conserve the fisheries, fauna and flora of the island", extensive efforts have been made to preserve the island's natural heritage. The Act declares that the whole island is protected from unlawful clearing, cultivating, grazing or mining, with fines imposed for trespass or damage. In 1981 the Act was amended to include the creation of a permanent park preserve covering untouched areas at the north and south ends of the island (some 70 per cent of Lord Howe).

In the same year these measures culminated in the NSW and Federal governments nominating LHI for the United Nations World Heritage List. Under the World Heritage Convention adopted by UNESCO in 1972, signatories to the convention are required to do everything possible to identify, protect and conserve their natural and cultural heritage for future generations. Properties considered to have "outstanding universal value from the aesthetic, scientific or cultural point of view" can be nominated for the World Heritage Register.

On 14 December 1982 the Lord Howe Island group was accepted onto the register – one of the smallest areas ever included on the basis of natural qualities. The only other Australian regions on the list at that time were the Great Barrier Reef in Queensland, Kakadu National Park in the Northern Territory and Willandra Lakes in western NSW. As Neville Wran, then NSW Premier, said: "Lord Howe Island and its surrounding islets and seas is an area of immeasurable importance, not only to the State, but also in world ecological terms."

GRAHAME McCONNELL

Exploring the land

Within an hour of touching down at LHI airport, many visitors have booked in to their accommodation and are out and about, enjoying breathtaking views such as those from 208 m high Malabar Hill or one of several other lookouts. With more than 20 km of well-marked tracks and tremendously varied terrain, Lord Howe offers bushwalks for all ages and abilities.

Because of its relatively small size, many scenic lookouts and diverse plants and animals, Lord Howe is best explored on foot. Just ambling along the roads and beaches is a pleasure, with different views and points of interest at every turn. Snakes, stinging plants, and hordes of tourists and biting insects – features often associated with tropical islands – are delightfully absent from LHI, and moderate temperatures make walking comfortable year-round.

As Lord Howe Island Board ranger Dean Hiscox says: "People really enjoy getting out on the tracks, and we're continually improving them to ensure visitor safety and enjoyment."

Well-marked tracks traverse much of the island, leading bushwalkers through a variety of forest types to lookouts, bird colonies, deserted beaches and remote rocky coves. Walks vary from an hour-long meander in Stevens Reserve to the challenging all-day trek to and from Mt Gower's summit.

Taking it easy

Transit Hill is an excellent walk for first-time visitors. Its central position and viewing platform provide 360° views, so it's a great place from which to identify landmarks. Starting near the administration office, the track gently climbs through typical Lord Howe dry forest, with trees such as blackbutt, maulwood and axe-handle-wood. After reaching the platform, the path descends to Blinky Beach, where walkers can return to their starting point by following Lagoon Road beside the airstrip. Allow two hours for this walk.

A two-hour-return stroll to The Clear Place from Anderson Road has much to enchant walkers, including views over Middle Beach, a dense kentia-palm forest and towering banyan trees. The palm forest shelters thousands of nesting flesh-footed shearwaters, best observed at dusk from September to April. Walkers must ensure they stay on the track to avoid stumbling into the birds' shallow burrows. The cacophony made by the shearwaters as they return from feeding on the open ocean continues through the night.

Once walkers reach The Clear Place, they're rewarded with views of the mountains and a glimpse of Balls Pyramid. In summer many seabirds cruise past; masked boobies, black-winged petrels, sooty terns and common noddies among them.

Walkers pass through grassy paddocks (above) on short strolls near Transit Hill. Longer walks – taking up to four hours return – to Boat Harbour and back, wind past green plum, hotbark and giant scalybark trees, whose sprawling buttresses engulf visitors like Jenny Roots (opposite left). Starting from Moseley Park, near Cobbys Corner, the two routes to Boat Harbour cross the island from west to east, through towering rainforest and other woodlands, bringing walkers to a beach (opposite right) of rounded black basalt boulders and white coral blocks. The secluded bay is ideal for picnics and swimming – its sheltered position is particularly sought after when strong winds whip LHI's western coastline.

Jims Point, on the rugged east coast between Neds and Middle beaches, is well worth a visit for those with an hour or so to spare. Follow McGees Parade to its eastern end, then walk through a grassy paddock onto the cliff edge near a large Norfolk Island pine. From the 50 m high cliffs, which fall to secluded coves and rock platforms, the Admiralty Islands are clearly visible to the north. To the south, Middle Beach's wave-cut platform invites exploration at low tide.

Another interesting walk loops through Stevens Reserve, starting near the visitor centre. The flat track, complete with interpretive signs providing information about plants, birds and history, passes through very tall lowland forests of blackbutt, maulwood and palm, with some superb examples of the spreading banyan. The reserve also contains a grove of eucalypts and three species of pine, which were planted in the 1930s to provide timber for building houses. They've never been logged because the mill was dismantled shortly after the trees were planted. Near the pines stands a laboratory building used in the woodhen-breeding program in the early 1980s.

Medium walks

The Boat Harbour track is probably the most interesting medium day walk on the island and is best tackled as a round trip. It starts near the airport around the eastern side of Intermediate Hill. After about 1 km a short track leads to a viewing platform overlooking the masked booby colony on Mutton Bird Point. Towards Rocky Run, the main track delves into a sheltered valley between Intermediate Hill and Mt Lidgbird where rainforest species such as blue plum, scalybark, island cedar and pandanus (or screw pine) abound. At the track's end, Boat Harbour provides a scenic spot for a picnic lunch and swim. The boulder beach is fun to explore and often has an interesting assortment of flotsam and jetsam cast up by the tide. Fresh water is always available at the harbour and at Rocky Run. Return via Lagoon Road near Kings Beach, using a connecting track that traverses Smoking Tree Ridge (so named because an old tree on the ridge was once a favourite smoko spot for those returning from a hard day's seed-collecting).

Breathtaking views of the southern mountains, the lagoon and the Admiralty Islands are seen from Malabar Hill's 208 m summit. Starting in the forest just behind Neds Beach, a steep track climbs a grassy paddock to Malabar Ridge. The ridge's stunted trees are an excellent example of an exposed dry-forest environment. Flowers of the orchid *Dendrobium macropus howeanum*, which grows on rocks and trees beside the track, are seen in August and September, and in December ground-orchid flowers of *Plectorrhiza erecta* appear beside the first 200 m of track in the forest. Malabar's summit is a terrific spot to observe seabirds in flight during spring and summer. The cliffs contain hundreds of nesting nooks for red-tailed tropicbirds and some visitors spend many pleasant hours observing their spectacular courtship flights. Return along the same track for a two-hour round trip, or complete the three-hour loop to Kims Lookout and Old Settlement Beach via the Max Nicholls Memorial Track.

In the island's north, many walkers take the rough, steep track over Dawsons Point Ridge to North Bay – a wonderfully secluded beach suitable for swimming, snorkelling and reef-walking. At low tide it's also accessible by boulder-hopping around the shoreline from Old Settlement Beach. Either way takes about an hour.

From the bay's picnic area – which includes tables, barbecues, shelter sheds and water tanks – several interesting excursions beckon. At Old Gulch, just 10 minutes away, the waves have rounded black basalt blocks and white coral skeletons into a boulder beach, and common noddies nest in bushes along the cliffs. At low tide, adventurous walkers continue around the eastern side of Old Gulch to Herring Pools, where fish and corals inhabit a number of delightful rock pools, some deep enough for swimming and snorkelling.

One of the best views on Lord Howe rewards those who take the strenuous 30-minute hike from North Bay's picnic area to the 147 m summit of Mt Eliza. It provides a glorious vista down to the beach and across the lagoon to the southern mountains. In summer, sooty terns can be seen nesting on or close to the track, and red-tailed tropicbirds gracefully soar by.

Harder hikes

Superb views back towards the north of the island are a feature of the steep climb to Goat House Cave, on the north-eastern side of Mt Lidgbird. For those keen to tackle the more challenging Mt Gower walk, the 400 m ascent on this three-hour return walk is a good opportunity to test fitness.

The Goat House track starts at the southern end of Lagoon Road beneath Mt Lidgbird. After climbing to Smoking Tree Ridge, it follows the brow of the ridge, growing steeper as it approaches the mountain. Higher up, the walk is quite thrilling, passing through an overhanging cave and requiring the use of fixed ropes in one precarious section. At the end, walkers have stunning views of Balls Pyramid and the rugged coastline behind Mt Lidgbird. Many of the island's rarer plants – such as the Fitzgeraldii tree, hotbark, mountain rose and the orchid *Dendrobium moorei* – only grow at these altitudes, as they favour the higher rainfall, humidity and exposure to wind.

Mt Gower

The ultimate LHI trek is undoubtedly to the summit of Mt Gower. An ascent more difficult than any other on the island, the eight-hour return trip should only be undertaken by the physically fit. The LHI Board also stipulates that all parties must be accompanied by an authorised guide.

After taking walkers through a great variety of terrain, scenery and vegetation,

Stunning views confront walkers on nearly every island track. From North Bay, a short steep climb to Mt Eliza's sharp summit provides panoramic vistas (above) across the lagoon to the southern mountains. On nearby Malabar Hill, which drops 200 m directly to the sea, wary cliff-huggers (opposite left) spy fish and turtles in the clear blue water. Five kilometres south, a coastal 4WD management track (opposite right) leads walkers from the end of Lagoon Rd, past Salmon Beach and Far Flats, to Little Island. The basalt cliffs of 777 m Mt Lidgbird tower above the track, and a constant swell rolls onto the boulder beaches at its base.

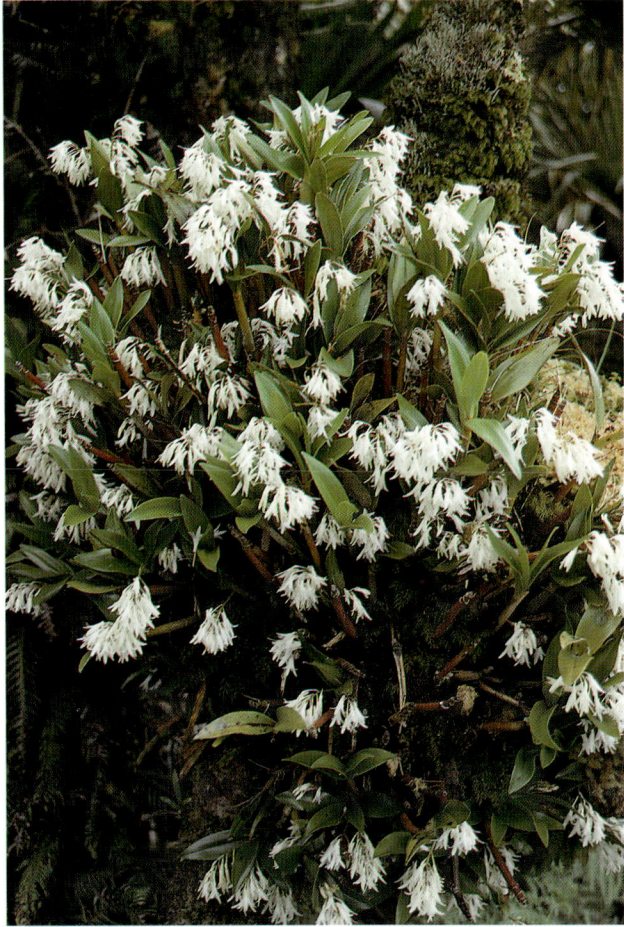

It's easy to see why names such as "Hobbit forest" and "primeval forest" are bandied about by first-time visitors to Mt Gower's stunted summit rainforest (opposite). Every tree, branch, rock and patch of ground is covered in a rich profusion of ferns and mosses. Sprays of delicate Moorei orchid flowers (above) cling to branches and tree stumps, and big mountain palms (right) thrust upwards, searching for sunny spaces in the canopy.

Pinnacle of Lord Howe bushwalks, Mt Gower's mist-shrouded summit (above) beckons the fit and adventurous. A solid four-hour climb rather than a walk, the Mt Gower track rises from sea level to an 875 m high apex, through ever-changing vegetation, past magnificent vistas and over obstacles such as Get Up Place (left), a cliff line about 700 m up. Along with the sense of achievement and satisfaction when the summit is reached, trekkers are rewarded with views north across the island (opposite above) past big mountain palms sticking out of the canopy, and a close look at the unique summit rainforest (opposite below) with its ferns, mosses, pumpkin trees, little mountain palms and pumpkin bushes.

the track climaxes on Mt Gower's summit with spectacular views of Mt Lidgbird, the lagoon and northern parts of the island. Local mountain guide Jack Shick says that people remark on two aspects of the climb: "First is the sheer challenge of the walk, 875 m almost straight up, and second the amazing diversity of vegetation as you climb higher, culminating in the mist forest on the summit."

Higher rainfall and humidity on the mountain top provide ideal conditions for the amazing profusion of mosses, ferns and orchids that festoon the trees and cover the forest floor. Guides usually stop in a small clearing at the summit where walkers devour their lunch beside woodhens and currawongs. The mountain top is clad in stunted, endemic rainforest plants like hotbark, pumpkin tree, green plum, little mountain palm and big mountain palm. From March to September providence petrels put on spectacular flying displays, swooping and soaring around the summit. Constant shouting and calling will induce them to land at your feet.

For those lacking the energy to scale Mt Gower, the walk as far as Little Island is well worth the effort. An old vehicular track provides access to the rugged coastal landscape beneath the towering basalt ramparts of Mt Lidgbird and it's easy to spend half a day exploring the area. Little Island, a large rock outcrop right on the shore, is a favourite subject for visiting artists and from March to September providence petrels amass there in late afternoon.

Island menagerie

Dazzling birdwatchers with their amazing courtship displays, red-tailed tropicbirds perform backward somersaults hundreds of metres in the air. Lord Howe is said to have the world's greatest breeding concentration of these graceful seabirds. During summer their aerobatics can be viewed around the southern mountains and along the cliffs from North Head to Malabar Hill.

Visitors to Lord Howe are often entranced by the island's most visible animals: thousands of birds – soaring overhead, nesting in huge colonies and strutting around the settlement and forest floors. But a closer look reveals a unique animal population that includes lizards, a bat species, freshwater fish and many invertebrates.

Animals that fly or are easily transported from one place to another, insects for example, are usually abundant on islands. Reptiles are also often found on remote islands as they are durable travellers. They, or their eggs, can withstand the drying effects of wind and salt water, and may be transported on logs washed into the sea. Land mammals and frogs, however, generally aren't good long-distance travellers, so tend to be absent from islands such as Lord Howe.

Of all the creatures that spend at least part of their life cycle on land, birds are best adapted to long journeys over the ocean and are among the best colonisers of islands. A total of 166 bird species have been recorded on LHI and 14 seabirds and 18 land birds are regular breeders there today.

Seabirds

Adapted to a life wandering the oceans in search of food, seabirds mostly come to land to breed, a process involving courtship, nest-building, egg-laying and the raising of young. At other times most seabirds travel the oceans, sometimes thousands of kilometres from their breeding grounds.

One of just two island groups in the Tasman Sea, the Lord Howe group is a haven for breeding seabirds and 150 years of human settlement has not greatly affected them. Natural mammalian predators have not reached its shores, so birds can breed in safety – and they do, in their hundreds of thousands. As Canberra-based seabird researcher and ecologist Dr Peter Fullagar says: "Lord Howe has an extremely rich population of seabirds, with more species breeding, in more spectacular numbers, than anywhere else in Australia."

The island is home to the world's only providence petrel breeding colony (apart from a few breeding pairs recently discovered on the Norfolk Island group), the only Australian breeding location for the Kermadec petrel and

Precious yet precarious. The white tern balances its solitary speckled egg (above right) in depressions on bare limbs of large trees like Norfolk Island pines. After 28 days' incubation, the hatchling (above) is closely guarded by one parent for the first week. Then its appetite grows so much that it's left alone while both parents seek food. Young masked boobies (opposite left) on Roach Island, 2 km north-east of Lord Howe, are also left alone while their parents make fishing forays great distances from home. Superb divers, the 80 cm long adults spear fish and squid up to 40 cm long on their pointed beaks. Other seabirds, such as flesh-footed and wedge-tailed shearwaters, head for their thriving colonies on LHI as the sun sends its last burst of light for the day to the west coast (opposite right).

grey ternlet, and the world's most southerly breeding sites for the sooty tern, common noddy and masked booby. It also has one of the world's largest breeding concentrations of red-tailed tropicbirds and the largest breeding population of flesh-footed shearwaters. Roads and marked walking tracks provide easy access to many of the LHI colonies and chartered boats regularly cruise close to offshore seabird colonies.

Many seabirds can also be seen around the settlement. The islanders' favourite is the exquisite white tern, which breeds along Lagoon Road, precariously laying a single speckled egg directly on a tree branch. As many of these "nests" are only 3 m above the ground, it's possible to sit quietly and observe the birds as they brood and rear their young. The best place to look is in the Norfolk Island pines between Lagoon Beach and the road.

Flesh-footed shearwaters breed in the forest behind Neds Beach. After feeding at sea from dawn they return in their multitudes at sunset and can be observed scuttling through the palms into their burrows. Every night from September to April their mournful calls resound from their forest home. At the southern end of the beach, black-winged petrels can be seen flying around the cliffs on summer days, often returning to their burrows hidden among bushes on the cliff face. After the eggs hatch in late February, the petrel colony may appear deserted, but the parents are still very active, slipping in at night to feed their chicks. Sooty terns –

the most numerous of Lord Howe's breeding seabirds – breed among the rocks towards the northern end of Neds Beach. Their numbers have increased since feral cats were removed in 1979.

From early afternoon the daily return of wedge-tailed shearwaters provides an engrossing spectacle around Blackburn Island, off Lagoon Beach. Small numbers of this common, sooty-brown bird also nest at a few locations on the main island including Signal Point, Lovers Bay and above Windy Point.

Malabar Hill is the best place to watch red-tailed tropicbirds in flight. Most active in the afternoon, they nest on cliff ledges from Malabar to North Head and perform their aerobatics quite close to the cliff face. In a fascinating courtship display, one of a pair will float with outstretched wings while the other – holding its body vertically – flutters backwards with rapid wing beats, arcing over its partner.

Further from the main settlement, Mutton Bird Point has a large colony of masked boobies. About 120 pairs of this 80 cm long seabird are present there year-round. Sooty terns, common noddies, grey ternlets and wedge-tailed shearwaters also nest on the point in smaller numbers.

Mt Gower and Mt Lidgbird are centres of seabird activity in winter, when providence petrels breed. On a still day, the noisy screeches of these birds are heard from the base of Mt Lidgbird, and they're seen flying near Little Island from March to September. Any persistent loud noise will bring them swooping down,

One of the most appealing aspects of Lord Howe is the ease of access to its seabird colonies, with many roads and walking tracks leading directly to them. If approached quietly, sooty terns (opposite above left), grey ternlets (opposite below left), wedge-tailed shearwaters (opposite above right) and little shearwaters (opposite below right) can often be observed at very close range. Many seabirds breed in dense colonies. At areas like New Gulch (above), at the foot of Mt Eliza, visitors are privileged to experience the sounds and sight of thousands of sooty terns, circling above and screeching to the chicks on the ground. Walkers should tread extra carefully near tern colonies as the nesting sites are often very close together.

and at Goat House Cave on Mt Lidgbird they'll even land at the feet of walkers. Red-tailed tropicbirds nest on the steep sides of both mountains during summer and are often observed cruising past.

On very calm summer days, boat-charter parties occasionally land at Roach Island in the Admiraltys. No visitor should miss the chance to experience Roach, one of the island group's largest seabird colonies, with thousands of sooty terns, masked boobies, common noddies, grey ternlets and wedge-tailed shearwaters. For keen birdwatchers, the four-hour boat trip to and from Balls Pyramid is also a must. Apart from this enormous spire's scenic splendour, it's the only known Australian breeding location for the Kermadec petrel and they can be seen wheeling high about the cliffs. Adult Kermadecs have dark-brown wings, but the body can vary from a dark grey-brown to near white.

Land birds

When discovered by Europeans in 1788, LHI had 15 species of land bird, of which 13 were endemic. Nine are now extinct. The white gallinule and the white-throated pigeon were hunted to extinction before settlement, the red-fronted parakeet was eliminated as a perceived pest and was last seen in 1869. A further five birds became extinct within a few years of rats arriving in 1918 – the vinous-tinted blackbird, the Lord Howe gerygone, the Lord Howe fantail, the robust silvereye

and the Lord Howe starling. The most recent disappearance was the Lord Howe boobook owl, last heard in the early 1950s.

The sacred kingfisher, woodhen, Lord Howe currawong, emerald ground-dove, Lord Howe Island white-eye and Lord Howe golden whistler are the only land birds to have survived the impact of humans. Twelve land bird species have become established on the island since 1788, most since 1920. They probably fill niches left vacant by the extinct birds, or have benefited from human modifications to the environment, such as the clearing of forest for pasture. Some of these newer arrivals – the masked owl and the magpie-lark – have been introduced, but others, like the eastern swamphen and masked lapwing, made their own way.

Of all the land birds, the emerald ground-dove is probably the most commonly seen. Appearing quite tame, it walks nonchalantly through the bush and often wanders close to roads. The colourful sacred kingfisher also captures visitors' attention, and it's frequently observed atop fences, keeping an eye out for worms and insects.

Walkers in lowland forests often hear the cheery songs of introduced blackbirds and song thrushes, and golden whistlers. These smaller birds, particularly the golden whistler, are often unafraid of humans and will venture into buildings in search of food. In the southern mountain area, walkers are often escorted along the track by Lord Howe currawongs, which observe all intruders with beady-eyed curiosity and can swoop aggressively at those passing near their nests.

Shot and clubbed to extinction by the mid-1850s, the endemic white-throated pigeon (above) is one of nine land birds no longer seen on the island. The vinous-tinted blackbird or ouzel (above left), which had evolved on the predator-free island, was wiped out after rats were accidentally introduced in 1918. It was known locally as the doctor bird because its colour matched that of a long brown coat worn by Dr John Foulis, one of the island's earliest residents. Thankfully, most seabirds – which generally only come ashore to breed – have fared much better than land birds, as shown by the thriving year-round masked booby colony (opposite left) at Mutton Bird Point and the black-winged petrel colony (opposite right) at Neds Beach. From November to March, petrel pairs perform spirited courtship displays around cliffs at the southern end of the beach.

The major celebrity and biggest success story among island birds is the woodhen, a brown, flightless bird about the size of a small chook. Once common in the island's subtropical rainforest, woodhens had no experience of predators, either human or animal, making them easy game for sailors and early settlers.

In 1788 surgeon Arthur Bowes Smyth of the *Lady Penrhyn* described the woodhen as "a curious brown Bird … walking totally fearless & unconcern'd in all parts around us, so that we had nothing more to do than to stand still a minute or two & knock down as many as we pleas'd wt. a short stick – if you throw'd at them and miss'd them or even hit them without killing them, they never make the least attempt to fly away …"

This hunting, combined with habitat disturbance and predation by pigs, cats and dogs, confined the woodhen to the southern mountains in vastly reduced numbers. An 1887 expedition to collect woodhen specimens on Mt Gower saw only one. The long-beaked birds were classed as endangered in 1966 and further research in the 1970s found that less than 30 survived and they were confined to the summits of the southern mountains. Urgent, positive action was required. Feral pigs and cats were eradicated and in May 1980 three healthy woodhen pairs were taken from the summit of Mt Gower to a breeding compound at Stevens Reserve. In one of the most successful projects of its type in the world, 92 chicks were raised and released over the next three years.

According to Dr Bob Harden, manager of the current monitoring program, the

population seems to have recovered and is near estimated maximum levels for the remaining habitat. "There appears to be a relatively stable population of about 220 woodhen on the island, with 50–60 breeding pairs. Although many more are known to have hatched since 1983, woodhen are territorial and adult males aggressively defend their territory, even from their own offspring."

Visiting birds

Several other bird species are regular visitors to LHI and can be seen at about the same time each year. The Pacific golden plover, whimbrel, ruddy turnstone and bar-tailed godwit breed in the Arctic, but winter in the Southern Hemisphere. They can usually be seen October–March, foraging along the rocky reefs and beaches at low tide, or feeding on mown grassy areas such as the airstrip verges. Double-banded plovers can also be seen in similar areas. These birds migrate to Australia from New Zealand for winter, and a few stop on Lord Howe.

   In winter and summer, cattle egrets are often sighted pacing elegantly beside grazing cows. These 50 cm tall birds, usually in groups of 3–4, stop en route from New Zealand to the NSW mainland. Many other migratory birds also briefly visit Lord Howe; the greenshank, red-necked stint, Japanese snipe and grey-tailed tattler among them. The best places to observe these irregular visitors are deserted beaches such as Old Settlement and North Beach, and the small swamp behind Blinky Beach.

Often heard in the lowland forest declaring its territory with a short sweet melody, the male Lord Howe golden whistler (above right) is probably the most vocal of the four surviving endemic land-bird species or subspecies that shelter in Lord Howe's forests. Another endemic, the tiny LHI white eye (opposite right), flits in small family flocks from branch to branch in search of insects, introduced pawpaw and other fruit-bearing trees, while Lord Howe pied currawongs (opposite left) watch passers-by with beady-eyed curiosity. Travelling from much further afield to escape the winter snows at their Arctic breeding areas, 40 cm high bar-tailed godwits (right) spend summer foraging on sand flats at low tide and around mown areas, looking for worms, molluscs, crustaceans and insect larvae. The long-billed birds begin their return trip north by March.

GRAHAME McCONNELL

Mammals and reptiles

Lord Howe's only native mammal is, not surprisingly, one that could colonise the island by flying there. On summer evenings, the large forest bat may be glimpsed flying erratically near bright lights. Less than 5 cm long and weighing only as much as a 50c piece, the furry insect-eater lives in hollow limbs or large cracks in trees. Skulls of another bat, the endemic LHI long-eared bat, have been found, but live specimens have never been seen, despite thorough searches.

The two lizard species – a gecko and skink both growing to a total length of about 16 cm – are now quite rare on the main island, but can often be seen on some of the offshore islands. Only found in the Lord Howe and Norfolk island groups, they hide in cracks in trees, boulder piles behind beaches or the honeycomb of small tunnels that riddle the soft calcarenite rock of the lowlands – locations that offer a safe place for egg-laying and exclude predatory rats. The skink has been observed feeding on bird eggs by rolling them over rocks until they break.

Since about 1995 the rainbow skink from eastern Australia has been seen in increasing numbers on the island, a matter of great concern. It was probably introduced with cargo from the northern NSW port of Yamba, about 220 km south of Brisbane.

Freshwater fish

LHI has no large streams, but there are many ephemeral runnels that flow after heavy rain and a number of small creeks, some of which contain permanent water. Two eel species inhabit these creeks: the short-finned eel, which varies in colour from golden-olive to olive-brown on top and greyish to white underneath; and the more common long-finned eel. Its back can range from a mottled olive-green to brown with paler sides and belly. Both eels are believed to spawn in the Coral Sea near New Caledonia, making a huge oceanic migration there when sexually mature at 10–35 years old. The tiny larvae are then transported south in the east-Australian current and may spend up to three years at sea before attempting to enter a freshwater habitat.

The common jollytail or spotted minnow, a small silver fish with mottled dark spots, lives in Soldier Creek in the island's south. A slender, active fish up to 15 cm long, it's widely distributed in the Southern Hemisphere. The adults spawn during spring tides, when the larvae are carried out to sea. They grow over winter and move back into freshwater streams in spring.

Other creatures

Because of their size, small animals without backbones, such as insects, spiders, worms and snails, are often overlooked. However, they play a vital role on Lord Howe: recycling nutrients in the leaf litter, pollinating flowers and providing a major food source for larger land animals such as lizards and birds.

GLENN A. HOYE

A large forest bat (above) – Lord Howe's only native mammal species – rests on a shiny green kentia frond. Weighing less than a 50c piece and only 5 cm long, the bat is the largest of its group, hence its seemingly incongruous name. Most vertebrate land animals have difficulty making long ocean crossings to colonise islands, but the bat's ancestors were able to fly to LHI from the Australian mainland. Eggs or breeding adults of the island's two lizard species – a gecko (opposite above right) and a skink (opposite below right) – probably arrived floating on logs. Both species have been preyed upon by rats, so are not common on the main island. They are more evident on offshore islets such as the Admiraltys (opposite left), where rats haven't become established.

Often undetected, small invertebrates such as spiders, insects and snails thrive on the Lord Howe group. The golden-orb weaver (above) is one of the more obvious of the 102 known spider species, its large webs regularly encountered by walkers in the forest. People keeping their eyes peeled might spy the round-shelled GUDEOCONCHA SOPHIAE *(above right) or one of 70 other endemic land snail species, although rats have taken their toll on some of these invertebrates. Lord Howe's most unusual invertebrate, the land lobster or giant phasmid (opposite above left), was exterminated by rats on the main island, but was rediscovered on Balls Pyramid in 2001. Endemic cicadas (opposite above right) still make their presence known, however, decorating trees and other rough surfaces with their discarded, brittle "shells". Inside fallen trunks witchetty grubs (opposite below right) – the local name for longicorn beetle larvae – carry out a form of interior decorating, chewing out a network of tunnels.*

Approximately 70 species of land snail are found on the island, most of which are only millimetres long. The two larger species have been greatly reduced in number by rats. The more common is *Gudeoconcha sophiae*, which has a round flattened shell 3 cm across. The 6 cm long, white, conical snail shells on the forest floor are those of *Placostylus bivaricosus*.

The most conspicuous of the island's 102 spider species – about half of which are unique to Lord Howe – is the golden-orb weaver. Seen in large numbers in the summer months, it fixes its golden, sticky webs across bush tracks. Another common spider of the lowland forest is the leaf-curling orb weaver and in the grasslands near the creeks and coastline the slant-web orb weaver predominates. The only spider on LHI known to be harmful to humans is the redback, which is found around the settled area and was probably introduced.

Lord Howe has one species of endemic cicada, the small, black *Psaltoda insularis*. For a few months from December, the noise from thousands of these insects can be quite deafening.

Many beetles and bugs are active throughout the summer months, especially at night. The most spectacular is a 6 cm long, brown longicorn beetle *Agrianome spinicullus*. Its larvae, called witchetty grubs by the islanders, live in tree trunks, devouring the wood. Many affected trees eventually topple after becoming greatly

DAVID ROOTS

weakened by a labyrinth of holes. Larger island birds such as woodhens, curra-wongs and kingfishers eat the grubs and can be seen foraging for them in decaying fallen logs. A smaller wood-boring grub metamorphoses into the eye-catching, bright metallic-green beetle *Lamprina latreillei*, often seen in summer.

All 24 butterfly species recorded on LHI are found on the Australian mainland and some on other Pacific islands. Certain species have only been recorded once and are obviously migrants that haven't been able to establish themselves, perhaps because their larvae require food unavailable on the island.

One of the most mysterious of the island's invertebrates was the giant phasmid or land lobster, a 14 cm long, wingless stick insect. Despite its large popluation it fell prey to rats, becoming extinct on the main island soon after their arrival in 1918. It did survive on Balls Pyramid where a recently dead specimen was photographed in 1965 by Sydney rock climber David Roots. Recent scientific surveys at night located live phasmids on Balls Pyramid in February 2001 and April 2002.

Visitors prepared to wait patiently beside one of the island streams are likely to see some of Lord Howe's interesting freshwater crustaceans. There is an endemic, 2 cm long, almost transparent shrimp and a long-legged crab which, with its brown-coloured shell only 1 cm across, is quite difficult to find. Biologists believe that the shrimp evolved from a brackish water species of eastern Australia.

Introduced animals

In common with many other islands around the world, LHI had a number of animals introduced to it by humans, with disastrous results. Captains of early whaling ships put pigs and goats ashore so there would be a supply of fresh meat. Mice were accidentally introduced in the 1850s. Cats and dogs were brought to the island by early settlers and feral cats eventually became established, roaming the forests and preying on birds and small animals. The greatest single disaster occurred in 1918, when rats were introduced after the *Makambo* ran aground.

The effect that intentionally introduced animals have had on local plants is considerable. The largest visible impact has been caused by – and for – cattle. Most cleared lowland areas are still used for cattle grazing, but there is some pressure to use the land for other purposes: buildings, palm plantations or reforestation with native plants.

Feral cats and pigs were finally eradicated from the island in the late 1970s through a hunting program undertaken by islanders and rangers. Goats were removed from the north hills in the 1970s and a program, now almost complete, began in 2000 to remove goats from the southern mountains.

In trying to remove or control these introduced animals, humans are attempting to compensate for some of the destruction the animals have caused. These efforts have been rewarded, particularly in regards to the native bird population, which has increased in recent years. Providence petrels are breeding lower down the mountains since the removal of pigs; little shearwaters were known to have only nested on the offshore islets in living memory, but have now recolonised places on the main island. The number of land birds has also increased, the most spectacular example being the woodhen. Such successes provide hope for the future preservation of Lord Howe's unique and diverse animals.

Flowing year-round and providing a welcome stop for mountain walkers, Erskine Run (opposite above) spills down fern-filled Erskine Valley between the two southern mountains. A little searching in its freshwater pools will reveal two small and unusual crustaceans – an endemic shrimp (opposite below left) and a crab (opposite below right) that is also found in streams of south-eastern Australia, New Zealand and Norfolk Island. Its eggs were presumably transported between these places on the feet of migratory birds.

BIRD OF PROVIDENCE

The penal settlement on Norfolk Island, 1000 km north-east of Lord Howe, often faced food shortages, particularly after HMS *Sirius*, which was carrying supplies, was wrecked in 1790. The garrison and convicts survived by slaughtering large numbers of providence petrels (hence the name), taking 171,362 birds from April to July of that year. The bird was extinct on Norfolk by about 1800 but continues to breed on LHI.

H. GRÖNWOLD/NATIONAL LIBRARY OF AUSTRALIA

Profuse plant life

There are probably few islands of similar size possessing so rich and varied a flora as Howe Island, handsome banyan and other trees, shrubs, palms, pandanus, and dwarf ferns growing everywhere in great abundance and luxuriance.

JOHN DUFF, COLLECTOR, SYDNEY BOTANIC GARDENS, 1882.

Boasting 184 species of native flowering plants, most with relatives in nearby lands, Lord Howe serves up a rainbow of small but colourful blooms. The blood-red mountain rose (opposite below left) and its rare yellow form (below right) are both unique to the island, as is the attractive wedding lily (above right). One yellow-flowering herb (above left) is so different to plants from elsewhere that it's been given the name LORDHOWEA INSULARIS.

More than a century after Duff wrote these words, the description is still very apt – at least 70 per cent of the island is covered in native forest. The 184 species of native flowering plants, 58 types of fern and 105 moss species thrive in the many different habitats from sea level to Mt Gower's summit.

Different habitats have variations in moisture, soil type, and sun and wind exposure, creating the conditions suitable for a variety of plants. In the sheltered valleys tall rainforests dominate, with some trees reaching 20 m in height and many other plants forming the understorey. Ferns and mosses abound in moist gullies, creekbeds and soaks; epiphytes (non-parasitic plants that are supported by growing on trees and rocks) grow almost everywhere including on rocky cliffs and scree slopes; and a few hardy shrubs and grasses persist on exposed, wind-blown cliffs.

Among small islands in similar latitudes, Lord Howe is rare in that it has sufficient elevation for the development of mist forest on its summits. Warm, moist air rises over the mountains, cooling rapidly and causing high humidity and precipitation on and near their summits. Many of the island's unique plants grow on or around these mountain tops, some producing colourful displays of red, white and yellow flowers.

Even in fine weather clouds often cloak the southern peaks, providing the extra moisture that enables rainforest to flourish on Mt Gower's 27 ha summit plateau. This miniature wonderland has a dense growth of small trees; an abundance of shrubs, palms and tree ferns up to about 4 m in height; and a low undergrowth of ferns and sedges. It's whimsically described by some tourists as "Hobbit forest", for it does put the visitor in mind of some fairy-tale land. Epiphytic ferns, lichens and orchids cover almost every available space on the trunks and branches of larger trees and ferns, and mosses cloak many trees, spreading in large cushion-like clumps on fallen tree trunks and any available space on the forest floor. Similar plants are found on Mt Lidgbird, but its summit is much smaller than Mt Gower's and the mist forest is not so well developed.

Nearly all of LHI's plants are related to those on New Caledonia, Norfolk Island, the Australian mainland and New Zealand, though most of the endemic species are related to plants

Thick with palm trees and dark-green foliage, Lord Howe's forests have a decidedly tropical appearance (above). Hidden in the greenery, large fruits add colour and interest for human visitors and an important food source for many birds. Kava (opposite above left) has 10 cm long spikes with numerous tiny peppery fruits; blue plum (opposite below left) has fruits 5 cm in diameter, each with one large seed; and the island apple (opposite below centre) produces bunches of golf-ball-sized brown fruits, each with four shiny black seeds. The two mountain palm species – little mountain palm (opposite below right) and big mountain palm (opposite above right) – are most easily distinguished by the size of their fruit: big mountain palms have larger, egg-shaped fruits about 5 cm long.

in New Zealand and New Caledonia rather than Australia. They are considered to be Lord Howe's more ancient plants as their ancestors probably arrived via the chain of island stepping-stones when sea levels were lower. As New Zealand plant palaeontologist Mike Pole says: "I've been studying fossils of plants that lived in New Zealand's North Island 8 million years ago, and the closest living relatives to those I've seen are growing on the summit of Mt Gower." All of Lord Howe's ancient endemics such as hotbark, native blackbutt, kava (a relative of the plant from which the drink is made) and pumpkin tree survive in the moist rainforest areas of the mountains.

In more recent geological times plants have migrated from the Australian mainland, helped by prevailing winds and ocean currents. The gene pools of these plant populations are similar or identical to those of the same species on the mainland and most are not considered to be distinct species. The island's drier, northern forests are mainly composed of these newer arrivals, along with a few small pockets of the older species. As the climate gradually becomes drier, the newer plants are likely to continue displacing older endemic plants.

Trees and other flowering plants

Attractive flowers and fruits embellish only a small proportion of Lord Howe's native plants. The forest canopy generally appears as a mosaic of greens and outstanding displays of colour are rare. However, a closer look reveals a profusion of plant forms including towering trees with massive buttressed roots, rope-like lianas climbing into the treetops, and palms with gracefully arched leaves and long spikes of single-seeded fruits.

The most conspicuous trees are the four endemic palms. Peter Green, a researcher from Kew Gardens and author of the official *Flora of Norfolk and Lord Howe Islands*, says: "Lord Howe might rightly be called the Isle of Palms because nowhere else does an island this size have such dense stands." Kentias and curly palms grow in lowland areas, while big mountain and little mountain palms put down their roots in the mountains. The highland species have seed clusters resembling bunches of grapes.

Other island plants produce fruits that look like the familiar cultivated varieties but are inedible. Examples include green plum, blue plum and black grape. The island apple sprouts brownish bunches of fruit resembling kiwifruit.

Banyans are probably the island's most unusual trees. They spread over extensive areas by dropping rope-like aerial roots from their branches. Each of these roots develops into a subsidiary trunk which in turn grows its own branches. In this way each banyan keeps spreading – one on The Big Slope covered a massive 2 ha (about four soccer fields) until a landslide destroyed it in 1998. As surveyor R.D. Fitzgerald wrote in 1869, "blending with others, they form grand amphitheatres of columns, arches and green foliage that fairly astonish and delight the naturalist".

Living in creekbeds, pandanus prop themselves up with arrays of strong roots that can withstand water torrents, even when the main stem rots. In a favourable, moist environment, they can grow to 15 m high, with roots beginning halfway up their trunks.

Some LHI trees and shrubs provide beautiful displays of colour when in flower: lignum vitae has large yellow pea-flowers that brighten the forest in winter; mountain roses provide massed displays of red spiky flowers throughout summer; and in December the large shrub *Corokia carpodetoides* is covered in tiny, bright yellow flowers. The 10 orchid species all have exquisite flowers, though many are small and need close scrutiny to be fully appreciated. The only endemic orchid is *Dendrobium moorei*, which has clusters of white, 1 cm long flowers and grows only above 300 m in elevation.

An unusual tree-sized heath plant, the Fitzgeraldii tree produces long flower spikes, covered with numerous small, white, tube-like flowers. Another "oversized"

GRAHAME McCONNELL

Forming tepees with their prop roots (opposite below), pandanus grow throughout much of the island's lowland forest, particularly along creeks and in other wet areas. The moist mountain environment supports most of Lord Howe's unique plants. Making up about one-third of the island's vegetation, the endemics are believed to have evolved from more ancient stock than most of the lowland plants. Perhaps they are relict populations of species that may have been more widely distributed in New Zealand or New Caledonia in past, wetter eras. Striking examples are pumpkin tree (opposite above), Fitzgeraldii tree (above), ALYXIA SQUAMULOSA *(above right) and* COROKIA CARPODETOIDES *(right).*

Sprouting from the forest floor, the brilliantly coloured fungus Secotium fragariosum *(top) compels curious observers to stoop and take a closer look. However, those who get too close to the starfish fungus* Asroe rubrus *(above) will doubtless experience its foul odour, thought to attract spore-spreading flies.*

plant, the pumpkin tree – a relative of the African violet – bears attractive orange flowers from October to April.

Striking white flowers are produced from July to November by the wedding lily, although each flower opens for only a day. The lily's only close relatives are found in southern Africa, so its appearance on LHI is quite a mystery. It may have grown on the southern supercontinent Gondwana and existed on the Australian mainland, dying out there at some time after it reached Lord Howe.

Fungi, lichens and mosses

Breaking down and recycling nutrients, fungi are found in Lord Howe's humid forests throughout the year, particularly after rain. They differ from most other plants in that they lack chlorophyll, taking all their nutrients from dead or living plants or animals.

Probably the most conspicuous fungi are the bright-red, button-shaped *Secotium fragariosum*, about 1 cm across, and a similarly sized blue-green species, *Weraroa novaezelandiae*. Both grow on dead palm fronds in the lowland forests. The brown ear fungus is also very common, growing on dead trees throughout island forests. Roughly resembling the human ear in shape, it has a velvet-like texture.

Some particularly unusual fungi glow brightly green at night, like tiny lights on the forest floor. The luminescence, produced by a chemical reaction involving oxygen and enzymes, may attract snails and slugs, which eat the fungi, in the process collecting spores on their body and so distributing them to new locations. One such fungus is the 2 cm round *Mycena chlorphos*, which sprouts from fallen trees in lowland forests after periods of rain. During the day it appears white and sticky.

With a white stalk up to 5 cm long and a crown of red, forked, horizontally spreading arms, the starfish fungus aids the distribution of its spores by producing a foul-smelling substance attractive to flies. After feeding on it the flies carry away spores both on and in their bodies.

Lichens are normally associated with the thin, dry vegetative coating on rocks and tree trunks, but one particularly striking variety is old-man's beard, a pale-green, hair-like species found dangling from the branches of trees on the cloud-shrouded mountain summits. Consisting of an alga and fungus growing together, lichens can flourish in difficult habitats where neither component could survive alone. They have encrusting, branched or leaf-like forms in many different colours that on Lord Howe make an attractive addition to the forest environment.

Mosses shroud almost every tree trunk and rock in the summit rainforest with a fine velvety cover. The island's 105 species are most abundant in moist areas, particularly near Mt Gower's summit. About 20 per cent are endemic, but this is considered a low figure when compared with other Pacific islands. Some 60 per cent are related to mosses in Australia, and many are also found in New Zealand.

GRAHAME McCONNELL

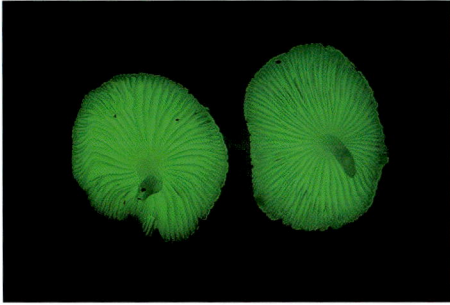

The island's rainforest (right) creates ideal conditions for mosses, ferns and lichens (above). Year-round, relative humidity varies little on LHI. It's generally in the 60–70 per cent range, but the onset of the Wet in northern Australia can bring days, or even weeks, of exceptionally low cloud, higher humidity and rain during summer. Rainfall is 15–20 per cent higher on mountain summits than the official meteorological readings taken from the middle of the island, and the damp conditions are ideal for a wide range of fungi, which play an important role in breaking down dead trees. Luminous fungi (top left) glow on the forest floor at night, possibly attracting insects and snails to feast on their fruit and spores, and velvety ear fungi (top right) are often seen sprouting from dead wood.

FERNTASIA

Adding a lush green to Lord Howe's subtropical rainforest are some of the island's 58 fern species, 23 of which are endemic. As ferns need moisture to complete their life cycle, it's hardly surprising that on LHI they're most abundant on the humid summits of Mt Gower and Mt Lidgbird. Some are restricted exclusively to these areas, particularly the filmy ferns *Cephalomanes* and *Hymenophyllum*, whose delicate leaf blades are only one cell-layer thick.

Although the small streams that flow from the mountains are also favoured fern habitat, not all ferns are found in damp, shady places. In pockets of soil on sunny rock ridges two species of resurrection fern thrive. They shrivel during drought, appearing to come to life again when it rains.

Lord Howe's ferns exhibit a fantastic variety of shape and form, ranging from the tiny *Ophioglossum reticulatum*, with a single frond a few centimetres long, to giant tree ferns with trunks up to 10 m high and arching fronds up to 2 m long. The four tree fern species are endemic and can be distinguished from one another by the shape and colour of the hairs on their frond stems. According to early reports, they were once particularly common around the foot of Mt Lidgbird, but were depleted as people collected them for the nursery trade in the late 19th century. Today they're found higher up the southern mountains.

Ferns familiar to many visitors include the tree-dwelling elkhorn, whose clumps grow to such a size that they sometimes topple the host tree, and the bird's-nest fern. The LHI bird's-nest has leathery dull-green fronds that are shorter and more erect than those on the Australian mainland.

One of the most attractive lowland ferns is *Asplenium milnei*. Bearing its spores in parallel rows on the undersides of its shining green fronds, it often sprouts from calcarenite rock. Walkers in the lowlands will also encounter *Phymatosorus pustulatis howensis*, which has divided, straplike fronds with tiny blister-like bumps caused by spore clusters on their undersides; and the climbing fern *Arthropteris tenella*. This fern has a creeping rhizome that enables it to scale tree trunks and rocks to a height of about 2 m.

Around Intermediate Hill and other lowland areas, the observant will find skeleton ferns, one of the oldest plant types on the island. These primitive ferns lack both roots and fronds, having bare green stems about 40 cm long and often dotted with small, yellow spore balls.

Cloud and canopy on Mt Gower's summit provide a natural shade house for more than 30 species of ferns – tall tree-ferns (opposite), 1 m high BLECHNUM HOWEANUM sprouting from the forest floor (top), and tiny epiphytic ferns like GRAMMITIS that clothe trees and branches (above).

Practical plants

Of all the island's plants, palms have been most useful to settlers. From the earliest days their trunks were split into battens for house frames and their leaves provided thatch for walls and roofs. By the late 19th century more substantial timber dwellings were being built, but palm thatch continued to be used in boatsheds and outbuildings until the 1940s.

The leaves were also woven into baskets, which were used to carry produce or suspended from the rafters to keep vegetables out of reach of marauding mice and rats. Decorative baskets were sold to passing tourist ships in the 1930s. Pandanus-leaf baskets have also been made for many years. The leaves are cut, dried and the edges stripped (to remove the sharp spines) before being woven into the durable baskets that are both used locally and sold to tourists.

The mat of stringy fibre that protects the growing heart of a palm was used in earlier times for a variety of purposes: stuffing for mattresses and pillows, protective packing for farm produce shipped to the mainland, tinder for fires and even as a precursor to toilet paper.

Scalybark, blackbutt and maulwood trees were sawn for timber, and the lignum vitae tree, which has particularly durable timber that resists rot and insects, was favoured for fence posts and foundation stumps for houses. Some local timber was also used for furniture making. One island joiner is said to have made a dining table and chairs from banyan timber, and the light wood of the island pine was used to make fish boxes.

Only a few native plants were used for food – probably the most accessible being "New Zealand" spinach, a herbaceous creeper growing in some shore areas. Islander Gower Wilson remembers his mother baking a "forkedy-tree pie" (pandanus were called forkedy-trees by some locals) from the edible seeds found inside the red fruits of the pandanus. Although regularly used for food in other parts of the world, the seeds were probably a curiosity rather than a regular dietary item on LHI.

Introduced plants

Many of Lord Howe's 218 introduced plant species were intentionally brought to the island for ornamental or farming purposes, such as the pasture grass kikuyu. Others were introduced accidentally, perhaps arriving with hay or general cargo. Fortunately, most are confined to the settled lowland areas, but some weeds have invaded the adjacent forests and are becoming a serious problem. To prevent more weeds reaching the island, the Board prohibits the importation of plants without permission.

The worst of the lowland weeds are two creepers, both known locally as asparagus fern, which produce fruits attractive to birds, thus spreading the seed further. Madeira vine and bitou bush are two other particularly noxious weeds. One tree species, *Pittosporum undulatum*, is also becoming a serious problem. Introduced onto the property Palmhaven around 1920, it's now spreading towards Transit Hill.

The southern mountain forests are under siege by Crofton weed and November lily. Botanists believe it's impossible to eradicate either as they're growing in remote, inaccessible areas. Cherry guava is also slowly spreading into many areas of the southern mountains, its seeds being distributed by birds. This species may become one of the island's worst weeds without concerted action to thwart its spread.

Brought to the island by humans, introduced plants pose a real threat to Lord Howe's World Heritage plant life. In recent years the Board has received some funding from the Federal Government to combat the threat and continued assistance is needed to keep weeds at bay. Future visitors may even be able to play a role in programs designed to counter the menace of introduced plants.

Crowded stands of kentia palms (opposite above) were a major source of building materials for island houses in the 1800s, and limited use of palm thatch for sheds (opposite below) and boathouses continued into the 1940s. As early as 1880, government conservation measures preserved hardwood trees such as scalybark (above left) and lignum vitae (above right) that might otherwise have been exploited for building. Today the biggest threat to LHI's native plant life is weeds – alarmingly, there are 218 species of introduced plants on the island. The integrity of forests is under threat from a number of aggressive weeds like asparagus fern (right), here being removed by volunteer Michael Crisp during an Australian Academic Tours expedition.

Sand and sea

Teeming with egg-and-sperm bundles, a bright-pink coral-spawn slick has been pushed by a southerly breeze into North Bay one warm February morning. The night before, many of The Lagoon's corals released their fertile packages, but the chance weather pattern means a lot will perish because winds have blown them ashore, not to open water. Some, however, will survive and form new coral larvae.

No sojourn on Lord Howe is complete without a close look at what must rank among its most spectacular attractions – the pristine waters and the life in them. Teeming with plants and animals, the ocean environment can be explored from boats or by snorkelling, diving or even walking on the shore.

LHI is separated from the Australian mainland by a 600 km expanse of the Tasman Sea. Twenty kilometres from the island, the water is 2 km deep, and roughly halfway between island and mainland the sea floor drops a further 2 km. The Tasman Sea is generally cool, but a warm current flowing down the east coast of Australia from north Queensland turns eastward at about the latitude of Lord Howe. Not only does this current transport eggs and larvae of tropical marine creatures to LHI, it maintains water temperature above the 17°C corals need, helping create the world's most southerly coral reef (apart from a small strip off Rottnest Island, WA). In summer, water temperatures around LHI can reach 26°C.

Australian Museum research scientist Dr John Paxton says this interesting meld of tropical and temperate waters has created a unique combination of marine life, with many fishes possibly being swept to the area as larvae from regions such as the Great Barrier Reef. However, most don't reproduce in the area. "The fishes of Lord Howe belong to a subregion that includes Elizabeth and Middleton reefs and, to a lesser extent, Norfolk Island," John says. "Although there are about 500 or so species of fish recorded there, many are present in very low numbers."

All of Lord Howe's marine life – from the swarming schools of kingfish and tuna to dolphins and 50-tonne humpback whales – rely on a food chain with lowly beginnings in phytoplankton. Floating near the ocean's surface, these microscopic plants are eaten by tiny animals (the zooplankton), which are in turn eaten by larger animals and so on up the food chain. One of the most conspicuous creatures in Lord Howe's zooplankton is locally known as brit. Billions of these shrimp, which are less than 1 cm long, swarm around LHI in spring. Fishermen tell of fish, engorged with brit, refusing to bite. Onshore winds sometimes blow brit onto the island's rocks or beaches, where they appear as long pink lines.

Beachcombing

Meandering along any of the island's 10 beaches, searching through the flotsam and jetsam delivered to the island by ocean currents and winds, is a rewarding way to start exploring the sea life around LHI. Attractive skeletons of marine animals are frequently found. The most commonly seen is that of the heart urchin – a hollow, flattened sphere up to 14 cm in diameter, with a star-shaped pattern on the top surface and a hole at each end. Another interesting object is cuttlebone – white, surfboard-shaped and commonly 10–30 cm long, it's the internal skeleton of the squid-like cuttlefish.

Occasionally the dead bodies of seabirds are washed onto the beach and their flesh is quickly stripped by scavengers like sea lice. Only millimetres long, these crustaceans come out at night to pick flesh from the bones of dead animals on the beach. Island fishermen take advantage of their activities by burying fish heads and scraps in the sand. Whole dead fish can often be seen washed up on the beach, especially the durable, squarish bodies of boxfish, which dry out like leather in the sun.

Very much alive, yellow-bellied sea snakes occasionally become stranded on beaches in rough weather. These dangerous air-breathing reptiles can survive out of water and are best left alone.

In late winter and spring, the beaches are sometimes coloured by thousands of bluebottles blown ashore by strong onshore winds. Careful searching among the

bluebottles, infamous for their potent stinging tentacles, will sometimes reveal other interesting animals, such as the by-the-wind-sailor with its disc-shaped body about 3 cm across. A triangular sail membrane sits atop the disc, and the animal has 1–2 cm tentacles – fortunately harmless to humans.

Shells of the violet snail are also occasionally washed up with these stingers. Floating just below the surface, suspended from a raft of bubbles secreted by gas glands in its foot, this garden-snail-sized animal preys on bluebottles, as do 2 cm long blue nudibranchs. With leg-like appendages on either side of their bodies, these nudibranchs are sometimes called sea lizards. Each appendage has finger-like projections that help the animals float on the surface. In an incredible feat of marine "recycling", blue nudibranchs make use of their prey's stinging cells, after relocating them to the tips of their own "fingers".

Along the tide line beachcombers will see numerous burrows up to 4 cm in diameter made by nocturnal ghost crabs. At twilight and during the night, the crabs scurry between their holes and the debris on the beach, carrying small pieces of dead plants and animals into their burrows. If approached, they quickly dart sideways into a hole or the water – whichever is closest.

Although not part of the natural environment, refuse washed up on the beaches is also a source of interest for visitors. Plastic buoys from torn fishing nets often find their way onto the island. In the past these buoys were made of glass and many feature as ornaments in some of the island's lodges and homes.

Sometimes logs, bottles and other floating objects are covered in white shells on fleshy stalks – goose barnacles. If the barnacles are still alive, return the object to the sea and watch the long thin legs emerge from the shell plates and wave through the water in search of food.

Rocky shores

Rising more than 2 km from the ocean depths, Lord Howe provides many marine habitats in which water depth, light intensity, anchorage points and nutrient levels vary, providing habitats for a diverse range of plants and animals.

The easiest way to observe this marine life is by exploring the island's rocky reefs at low tide. Neds Beach is the best area to start as it's easily accessible and its southern rock platform probably has a greater variety of marine life than the island's other intertidal areas. Some of the most prominent animals encountered are sea cucumbers – thick, slug-like animals up to 30 cm long. If prodded or picked up by predators they extrude numerous white sticky threads from their rear, which entangle and distract the attacker. Black sea cucumbers are the most common, but attractive orange and brown-and-white spotted species are also found.

The most active predator in these shallow pools, the seven-armed starfish *Astrostole insularis*, could aptly be called the terror of the intertidal zone. It eats mussels, small crabs, snails and slugs by extruding its stomach over its prey, or

Wind and waves regularly toss all sorts of creatures onto island beaches, providing hours of leisurely beachcombing. Ghost crabs about 4 cm wide (opposite right) scuttle about the beaches scavenging around thousands of delicate but dangerous by-the-wind-sailors (opposite below) driven ashore in late winter. Visitors fortunate enough to see yellow-bellied sea snakes (opposite middle) should leave them well alone. The venomous reptiles feed mainly on surface fishes, but may be harmful to humans. Other interesting beach finds include prickly heart urchin skeletons (opposite above), long-stalked goose barnacles (top) – which attach themselves to almost any floating object – and violet snail shells (above).

even into its body cavities. Up to 18 cm across, this starfish has blue or brown arms covered in short spines.

Walkers at Neds Beach often hear clicking noises from beneath the rocks. The sound is made by pistol prawns clicking their one enlarged nipper and may be a tactic to stun nearby prey. A range of other small animals shelter under rocks in shallow water. These include brittle stars, sometimes called sea serpents because of the snake-like movements of their arms. When disturbed by a predator they can break off their own limbs to effect an escape. Pink and grey bristle worms may also be sighted on the sandy bottom. Up to 6 cm long, the worms have hundreds of tiny bristles down each flank that can cause irritation if they pierce your skin. As with most animals, it's best to follow the "look but don't touch" rule.

The rocks themselves often have a bright film of deep blue, yellow, orange and black on their undersides. Known as an artist's palette, this film is composed of soft, encrusting sponges. Acting as tiny seawater filters, sponges such as these feed on very fine particles of suspended organic debris.

Some 200 alga species have been recorded around LHI. Some of the more striking are sea grapes – which resemble clusters of tiny grapes, each "fruit" only a few millimetres across – and bright-green sea lettuce. Both can be washed and eaten and are quite nutritious – the sea grapes are actually quite tasty. Another alga, dark-green turtle weed, grows as long hair-like filaments in round clumps to 40 cm

A delight to explore at low tide, Lord Howe's rocky shores contain a host of colourful marine life. Sponges (above) encrust the undersurface of many shoreline rocks, and seaweeds such as sea grapes (top right) decorate shallow pools in many shapes and shades of brown, red and green.

One particularly stunning marine landscape to explore on foot is The Potholes, a thick coral-rubble bank offshore from Far Flats. It's dissected by deep trenches that are only exposed a few times of the year at the very lowest of tides. Visitors can peer down into the clear underwater gorges to see corals and algae lining the walls and colourful fishes swimming over the white sandy bottom.

By running fingers through turtle weed's silky filaments, visitors are likely to tease out a bright-green crab (above) that matches the colour of its home. With similarly superb camouflage, light-blue crabs (opposite above) meld with the soft coral, blue xenia. Like many crustaceans, these crabs live in a symbiotic – mutually beneficial – association with their host. The crabs eat parasites and other small animals that attack the weed or coral in which they live. Beautifully coloured corals abound in shallow waters around the island. The pink hard coral (above right) is one of many that can be seen by reef walkers in rock pools, but the bright-red gorgonian corals (opposite below) live deeper, in the domain of scuba divers. Dark basket stars and feather stars use gorgonians as a platform to reach higher into the water column with their feathery tentacles as they trap food drifting past.

diameter. The alga is home to bright-green *Caphyra rotundifrons* crabs. About the size of a dollar coin, they've developed small hooks on the tips of their legs to help them cling to this constantly swaying weed.

Corals are abundant in LHI's rock-platform pools. Those called hard corals consist of a colony of hundreds of tiny polyps, animals which secrete a hard calcium-carbonate skeleton. These skeletons form the structure of coral reefs. If you run your hand over coral during the day, when the polyps have retracted, the colonies feel hard, but at night the feeding polyps extend their fleshy tentacles and the texture is quite soft. At Neds Beach, plate and brain varieties are the most common hard corals, but there are also smaller populations of the very fragile branched corals.

All corals gain nutrients in two ways: from photosynthesising algal cells embedded in the colony and by feeding on zooplankton. Each polyp's tentacles are armed with nematocysts – microscopic stinging cells that spear tiny animals and take them to the polyp's mouth.

In soft corals, polyps have no hard skeleton in which to retract. Coloured green, brown, blue and purple, these colonies often have the appearance of miniature flowers or cauliflower, with a dozen or more flower-like polyps protruding from a thick, fleshy stalk, and many stalks joined as one colony. In still water, each polyp can be seen with its star-shaped pattern of eight feeding tentacles around the mouth. One of the most striking soft corals is the blue xenia, so named because of its vibrant blue tips. It grows in intertidal pools in clumps up to 40 cm across. Run your fingers through a colony of blue xenia and you may tease out the 2 cm blue-and-white round crab *Caphyra laevis*.

Coral researcher Vicki Harriott, from Southern Cross University in NSW, says that many Lord Howe corals have a precarious existence. "The island features a small number of common species that specialise in subtropical locations such as Moreton Bay [southern Queensland] and a larger number of more tropical species. These tropical corals seem to come and go over time. Small numbers of larvae survive the trip down from the tropics, form coral colonies, live out their lives and then die out."

Colourful skeletal fragments of organ pipe coral decorate tidal pools and beaches. Covered in fleshy polyps when the coral is living, the bright red skeleton, composed of parallel tubes that look like organ pipes, is revealed once the polyps die.

On a few dramatic nights each year, usually about 9–10 nights after a full moon in January or February, nearly all the corals around Lord Howe reproduce, the polyps expelling eggs and sperm in pink bundles that float to the surface. If strong onshore winds are blowing, a smelly spawn slick will be visible along the beach the next day.

During summer, spectacular slug-like nudibranchs appear in the shallow waters in an almost endless variety of shapes and colours. Dorid nudibranchs have a circle of feathery gills at their tail and two stout tentacles that stand out from the back of their head. Aeolid nudibranchs, such as sea lizards, have clusters of finger-like appendages down each side of their body. The most spectacular nudibranch in LHI's waters, often seen at the ocean end of North Bay, is the spectacular, bright-red Spanish dancer, which grows to about 20 cm.

One animal that you have to look hard to see in shallow pools at North Bay and elsewhere is the sea hare. About 15 cm in length, this mottled brown animal derives its name from the two tentacles extending from its head. Another camouflage expert, the decorator crab, thrives in seaweed in the bay, matching its colour, leg and body structure to the surrounding weed. Some also attach small pieces of sponge or seaweed to their body to add to the disguise.

Tumbling over rocks when disturbed, hermit crabs – the clowns of the island's rock platforms – have tiny legs projecting from a wonderfully varied assortment of shells. These squatters take up residence inside the shells of dead sea creatures such as marine snails.

In North Bay's deeper pools many large orange-tipped sea urchins live mouth down, scraping algae off the rocks with their five long teeth. The 5–8 cm spines of this common urchin aren't poisonous but can penetrate a sandshoe. Gently pick one up and you'll feel it use them to "walk" across your palm. However, beware of the needle-spined urchin, distinguished by its 15 cm long, brittle, black spines.

JEFF DEACON

Underwater armoury. To protect themselves from predators, each of these marine creatures has a tried-and-tested strategy. The aptly named mosaic eel (opposite) deters would-be attackers with an impressive array of needle-like teeth, while the sharp spines on sea urchins (below right) repel all but the most ardent predator. Hermit crabs (below left) attach anemones to themselves for protection and decorator crabs (middle left) affix pieces of sponge and weed to improve camouflage. Sea cucumbers (above left) eject white sticky threads to entangle an attacker and the sea slug CYERCE NIGRICANS (above) exudes noxious secretions from its leaf-like appendages when provoked. Antithesis of stealth, the Spanish dancer nudibranch (above right) warns of its poison flesh with bright colours that intensify when it's alarmed and swims away by vigorously undulating its body – quite the opposite of the sea hare (middle right), which takes advantage of its in-built camouflage.

These spines can cause pain for several hours. Another dangerous rock-platform inhabitant is the textile cone. White with an orange scribble pattern and about 7 cm long, it's one of at least nine species known to be deadly to humans. About a quarter of all people poisoned by cone shells have died. All cones, which are types of marine snails, produce toxins to paralyse their prey, so they should be avoided or handled with extreme care. Less dangerous marine snails include the large green or orange turban shell, *Turbo cepoides*, a species found only at LHI and Elizabeth and Middleton reefs.

On the sea-sprayed calcarenite cliffs beside the rock platform at Neds Beach lives another group of snails, safe from water predators. The most common are black nerites, limpet shells and conniwinks. All use a rasp-like organ, the radula, in their mouths to scrape algae off the rock, wearing the rock so that it has a sharp, angular appearance.

At Middle Beach, marine erosion has reduced a mass of calcarenite rock to a terrace-like platform decorated with a lattice of pools, most of which contain water only a few centimetres deep at low tide. The platform is covered in a mat of algae – home to many microscopic animals. One peculiar inhabitant is the shady urchin, which picks up pieces of weed, rock and shells with its tubed suction feet, and places them on top of its body.

More common at Middle Beach than at other shore areas are two strombus

species – the 2 cm long flower stromb and the larger red-mouthed stromb. These acrobats possess a strong muscular foot with a horny claw-like projection that they use to lever their body along the rock. If knocked over, they flick out the foot to right themselves.

Hundreds of colourful burrowing clams are a feature of the large reef exposed at low tide near Little Island at the foot of Mt Lidgbird. Perched upright on the platform, the clams feed by opening their two shells slightly and pumping water through their bodies. Minute hairs on their gills filter out organic material. If disturbed the clams spurt a jet of water up to a metre into the air – a diversion that usually buys them enough time to close.

The reef's northern section presents some dramatic features, such as marine erosion trenches up to 5 m deep by 40 long and 10 wide. Known locally as The Potholes, the trenches are only exposed at the lowest tides and have abundant weed on their walls, providing a sheltered home for many fish.

An area well worth exploring at low tide is the outcrop called Far Rocks, jutting out south of Signal Point. These eroded calcarenite rocks are easily reached from the northern end of Lagoon Beach. The sand-covered platform's deep pools are home to some beautiful hard and soft corals and contain many colourful fish, including the poisonous butterfly cod, which glides through these pools with an amazing array of wing-like fins.

Standing knee-deep in clear, calm water off Neds Beach (left) while fish swarm for food is one of the special ways visitors can get a close look at Lord Howe's marine life. A host of sea creatures can be encountered simply by walking along the shore, among them hard-shelled marine snails, which abound between the low- and high-tide levels. They have ruthless killers and clever acrobats in their ranks. The red-mouthed strombus (above) can flick itself over with the horny claw on its muscular foot; and the knobby spine shell THAIS ARMIGERA *(opposite right) kills other snails by sitting in the shell opening and suffocating the occupant. For a closer view, snorkelling at Middle Beach in just a metre or two of water (opposite left) is one of the most rewarding beach experiences imaginable.*

Snorkelling

Slipping quietly into the water with a snorkel and face mask will take you closer to some of the 500 or so fish species and many other marine creatures recorded in Lord Howe waters. Top locations for beach snorkelling include Neds Beach, Middle Beach, Sylphs Hole and North Bay. Glass-bottomed boats regularly take snorkellers to Comets Hole, Erscotts Hole and North Bay, excellent spots in the lagoon. All locations offer beautiful coral outcrops, surging stands of algae and many colourful sponges, snails and other invertebrates.

Two endemic fish species that snorkellers are likely to encounter are the anemone or clown fish and the double-header wrasse, a blue-grey fish growing to 80 cm. Its name comes from a prominent bump on the front of its head above its eyes. Strong, pointed, protruding teeth enable the double-header to prise shells, crabs and urchins off the rocks. Growing to about 11 cm, the clown fish is black and white and is often seen hiding among the stinging tentacles of anemone clumps. Chemicals in its mucous coat help it withstand the anemones' poison so it can swim and feed in and around them, quickly disappearing among their tentacles if a predator approaches.

Diving

Those keen to travel deeper can strap on scuba gear and immerse themselves in the world of fish, where they'll encounter varied marine habitats. "The underwater terrain is spectacular," says local divemaster Jeff Deacon. "The varied rock formations include gutters, canyons, overhanging ledges and underwater plateaus. The most favoured destination is the Admiralty Islands, as they have a steep drop to a submerged plateau with prolific fish life." Sea caves extend back into the rugged cliffs in the island's north-east.

Because of the strong tidal currents around Lord Howe it's best to dive with assistance provided by a local dive-boat operator. If you want to learn to dive with scuba gear, island operators will provide a certified course of instruction over several days. "We also offer an introductory dive in the lagoon for people who just want to get a taste of it," Jeff says.

Surrounded here by dozens of moon wrasse, the double-header wrasse (opposite) – endemic to the region – is one of the largest fish that snorkellers and divers encounter off Lord Howe. More than 500 fish species are known from island waters, with semi-circular angelfish (right) and many other tropical species providing spectacular underwater colour. The coral reef provides shelter and food for a host of tropical marine creatures, including the nocturnal painted crayfish (above right), its beautifully decorated shell providing a protective screen in the coral.

PHOTOS: KEVIN DEACON

MIDDLETON AND ELIZABETH REEFS

Some 200 km north of LHI lie the world's most southerly coral atolls – Elizabeth and Middleton reefs. Influenced by the same ocean currents as LHI, these kidney-shaped reefs, both about 8.5 x 6 km, share its unusual blend of both temperate and tropical marine life, but being further north, they have more tropical elements – 122 coral species have been recorded at the reefs compared to about 85 at Lord Howe. The two reefs were once islands, but they're older than Lord Howe so have been eroded for longer.

Their lagoons are shallow – in most areas no more than 1–2 m deep at low tide. Encircling these are 100–200 m wide reef crests known as algal pavements. Made of coral rubble that has been cemented into a solid mass by specialised algae, the pavements have been worn smooth on top by the constant action of pounding waves and are safe to walk on at low tide.

A stunning labyrinth of blue holes up to 30 m deep lies at the heart of Elizabeth Reef's lagoon. The edges of these holes contain corals that are actively growing, some forming huge, spectacular walls. On the reef's western side a sand cay emerges at low tide, its sand formed from the ground-up skeletons of reef organisms.

The two reefs provide a significant food source for migrant seabirds including sooty terns, masked boobies, petrels and shearwaters. They often roost on the many shipwrecks or large coral-encrusted boulders around the algal pavement. Common noddies have also been observed breeding on the rusting hulk of *Fuku Maru No. 7* at Middleton Reef.

Forty-seven boats have been wrecked on the reefs, at the cost of at least 56 lives. In his report to the Australian Museum in 1936, fish researcher Gilbert Whitley wrote that the reefs "became known as grave-yards of the Pacific, for wreck after wreck was piled upon their coral, and derelict vessels from miles away were converged by currents upon these treacherous shoals". From 1800 to 1911, 24 ships met their fate there. There's little trace of these mainly wooden vessels, but remnants of the steel-hulled *Annasona* and *Errol* lie strewn across the reef crest at Middleton. Surprisingly, no further wrecks were recorded until the freighter *Runic* struck Middleton Reef in 1961. Since then, 18 fishing trawlers, three small yachts and the *Island Trader*, a small trading boat from Lord Howe, have come to grief on the atolls.

No regular trips go to the reefs – only adventurous sailors with their own vessels can visit this spectacular nature reserve. Under favourable conditions small boats can enter the lagoons of both reefs through chan-nels, but Middleton has a safer channel and larger anchorage. Coral out-crops are numerous in both, so navigation is difficult at low tide.

Its shallow aqua lagoon daubed with dark blue, indicating 30 m deep holes, Elizabeth Reef (above) rises from the Pacific 160 km north of Lord Howe. Vessels (opposite above right) carry adventurous sailors to Elizabeth and nearby Middleton Reef (opposite above left), enabling the seafarers to enjoy their beauty and isolation. Gazetted as a Marine National Nature Reserve in 1987, the reefs share similar geological origins and marine life with LHI. Their jagged coral edges have snared no less than 47 ships, the largest being RUNIC (opposite below), which ran full steam onto Middleton Reef in 1961 and is slowly being broken up by the seas that pound the reef at high tide.

Offshore islands

Spectacular eroded remnants of the original shield volcano abound both above and below the water around Lord Howe. Some are visible from the island, others can only be seen from a boat. Many are inaccessible, although in calm weather landings are possible at a few.

Semi-submerged rocks play a Jekyll-and-Hyde role in the island's maritime scene. They support much marine life, including encrusting corals and seaweeds, small reef fish and schools of bluefish, trevally and deep-sea kingfish, but they've been the nemesis of many passing ships. George Rock, to Mt Gower's south-east, and Wolf Rock, 2 km east of Boat Harbour, claimed ships in 1830 and 1837 respectively, and Mokambo Rock, 20 m north-east of Soldiers Cap, was named for the trading vessel that hit it in 1918.

The Lord Howe group's 27 exposed rocky islets total about 85 ha and are included in the World Heritage Area. Some are no more than rocks awash at high tide, but others are significant seabird rookeries with fascinating ecosystems. If the seas are not too rough, several of Lord Howe's boat owners will take interested visitors to the islets.

"There's certainly an element of risk involved in getting out to the islets," says ranger Dean Hiscox. "Apart from Blackburn Island in the lagoon, visitors need to arrange with locals to take them out and permission must be sought from the Lord Howe Board if you want to land on the islets."

The Admiralty Islands

Lying within 2 km of the northern tip of the main island, the Admiralty group has eight rocky outcrops – Soldiers Cap, Sugarloaf Island, Noddy Island, South Island, Roach Island, Tenth of June Island, North Rock and Flat Rock. Named Admiralty Rocks by Lieutenant Lidgbird Ball in 1788, the islets were given individual, descriptive names by subsequent generations of islanders.

All of these basalt islets – except Flat Rock – are characterised by steep-sided cliffs, rounded tops and volcanic dykes. In summer, tour-boat cruises regularly pass the Admiraltys and, when conditions are exceptionally calm, boat operators land visitors on Roach Island to witness the extraordinary spectacle of thousands of nesting seabirds. In the past, Roach Island's birds have

provided more than a spectacle. Guano was gathered there for fertiliser in 1881, and every year from the early days of settlement until the 1960s islanders gathered sooty tern eggs. Eaten fresh or preserved in salt for later consumption, the eggs made a protein-rich addition to the islanders' diet. One early account describes gathering up to 600 dozen eggs in a day. Fortunately, sooty terns usually lay another egg if they lose the first, so this egg-gathering didn't destroy the population.

Some 700 m long and 73 m high, Roach Island is the largest of the group. At its northern end, a spectacular tunnel passes from one side to the other at sea level. Water continually surges through this tunnel, but on calm days islanders have been known to motor through it in small boats.

Back from its cliffs, the islet is covered largely with tufts of hardy grasses like *Poa poiformis* and *Cyperus lucidus*. Herbs such as New Zealand spinach and *Lepidium* are also common. On the more sheltered north-east end, stunted trees and bushes grow – mostly tea-tree, sallywood, cottonwood and greybark. All are less than a metre in height, owing to frequent lashing by salt-laden winds and gales.

In spring and summer Roach swarms with tens of thousands of breeding seabirds, many of which will allow visitors to approach within a few metres of their nests. Eight species between them utilise every available cliff ledge, grass tussock, bush and patch of soil – masked boobies, sooty terns, grey ternlets, brown noddies, little shearwaters, wedge-tailed shearwaters, white-bellied storm petrels and a few

Centrepiece of the eight Admiralty jewels crowning the seas to Lord Howe's north (left), Roach Island is summer home to tens of thousands of breeding seabirds. Its smallest inhabitant, the 20 cm long white-bellied storm petrel (opposite left), nests in cavities among loose rocks, but the adults, who search for food day and night, are rarely seen ashore during the day, unless sitting on their solitary, speckled egg. Dive operators (opposite below right) regularly make trips to the Admiraltys so their clients can explore the many interesting coral-encrusted formations in the crystal-clear water. Dome-like Soldiers Cap (opposite above right) is the closest of the Admiralty group to Lord Howe, and from Malabar Hill observant walkers spy stunted bushes – sallywoods, melaleucas, greybarks and cottonwoods – growing in the grass near its 37 m summit.

red-tailed tropicbirds. Land birds from the main island also visit Roach, including magpie-larks, white-faced herons and nankeen kestrels. They are attracted by an abundance of food – grasshoppers and other insects – especially in autumn. Waders such as the ruddy turnstone, whimbrel and grey-tailed tattler visit the islet's rocky shores at low tide to forage for crabs and other small marine creatures.

In Sugarloaf Passage, which separates Roach from the north-east tip of the main island, the most striking feature is Soldiers Cap, named for its resemblance to the hats worn by some 19th-century British and French troops. In calm weather it's possible to land on the Cap's western end and scramble through stunted scrub to the top, 37 m above sea level, where small numbers of wedge-tailed shearwaters, common noddies and sooty terns breed, along with a few masked boobies. Terns and boobies also breed among the poa grass on South and Sugarloaf islands, north-east of Soldiers Cap. Perhaps the hardiest of the Admiralty group's seabirds are the grey ternlets and sooty terns that roost on Noddy Island to the west of Roach, even though the continual salty spray prevents vegetation from growing there.

About 1 km north of Roach, the swell washes continuously onto the base of North Rock, making landing dangerous. This imposing, 43 m high basalt outcrop is easily identified by its conical shape. Adjacent to it is the northernmost Admiralty – low, barren Flat Rock. The deep water around these two outcrops is popular with scuba divers because of the many interesting underwater rock formations.

With dark-brown wings outstretched, the Kermadec petrel (above) is often seen gliding leisurely near its only known Australian breeding location – the upper cliff ledges of Balls Pyramid. Eleven seabird species nest on the pyramid, including common noddies (top), which make their homes in the stunted bushes that cling precariously to cliff sides.

Balls Pyramid

An awe-inspiring tower of rock rising vertically out of the sea, Balls Pyramid dominates the skyline 23 km south-east of LHI. Rising to 551 m above sea level, it's magnificently coloured – dark-grey basalt tinged with the red stain of iron oxides, green vegetation and white streaks of guano. An early visitor, William Clarson wrote in the *Illustrated Sydney News* in 1881: "Viewed from the west in sunshine it presents the appearance of a massive golden spire; while, seen from the north-east, it resembles the dome of the Panthéon in Paris."

Named after its discoverer, Lieutenant Ball, who sighted it on his way to Norfolk Island, Balls Pyramid was probably once at least 6 km in diameter, but it's now 1100 m x 400 m at the base. It's thought that the volcano responsible for the rock's formation was active at the same time as the Lord Howe volcano, although the existence of a submarine trench between the two islands indicates that they were never physically linked above water.

Waters around Balls Pyramid are alive with schools of fish, particularly deep-sea kingfish, and in calm weather it is one of the islanders' favourite fishing spots. Its rock ledges are home to a great variety of seabirds including sooty terns, wedge-tailed shearwaters, red-tailed tropicbirds, black-winged petrels, white-bellied storm petrels, black and brown noddies and grey ternlets. The pyramid is also the only known Australian breeding location for the Kermadec petrel. Nesting high on the open ledges, this attractive seabird is often seen in flight during spring and summer, its breeding season.

Other islands

Of the other islands visible from the main island or from boats, one of the most accessible is Blackburn Island, located in the lagoon about 800 m from Windy Point. It has low cliffs on all sides, except in the south-east, where it slopes down to a shingle beach and a small sand spit exposed at low tide. This is the best place to land in a small boat, although on very low tides some people wade across the sandbar from Lagoon Beach.

Originally named after David Blackburn, sailing master of the *Supply*, this 2.5 ha islet's name was changed first to Goat Island, then Rabbit Island and finally back to Blackburn in 1973. When visiting the oval-shaped, grassy island, it's best to stick to the marked track to prevent damage to shearwaters' shallow burrows – the island is one of the principal breeding locations for the wedge-tailed shearwater. The birds lay their eggs in early summer and chicks hatch in January. Within three months the chicks fledge and migrate with the adults, possibly to the Northern Hemisphere.

Blackburn Island is the most likely place to encounter LHI's two lizard species. Only persistent searching under stones will reveal them during the day, but at

ON THE BALL

Balls Pyramid is listed in the *Guinness Book of Records* as the tallest "stack" in the world, a stack being the eroded remnant of a former coastline or island. Its awesome height, shape, spectacular location and resident wildlife have lured scientists and rock climbers for decades.

The first person believed to have landed on Balls Pyramid – in 1882 – was Henry Wilkinson, a geologist with the NSW Department of Mines. However, it is believed the first full-scale attempt to climb it didn't take place for another 82 years, when a group of Sydney rock climbers made a four-day assault on the summit, abandoning their attempt after running short of food and water. The following year another Sydney team, led by John Davis, reached the top. Since then a number of parties have successfully scaled the pinnacle.

In June 1979, AUSTRALIAN GEOGRAPHIC founder Dick Smith formally claimed the pyramid for Australia – an official act that had apparently been overlooked by the early explorers. Accompanied by veteran climber John Worrall, Dick was dropped by helicopter into the sea adjacent to the pyramid on 20 June. The two swam ashore and then climbed to a narrow ledge, where they prepared a base camp. Dick, John and climber Hugh Ward made the ascent to the summit the following day, where they unfurled the NSW flag – a gift from then State Premier Neville Wran.

"It's not the most difficult climb in the world," Dick said, "but the exposure is so fantastic, especially the sheer drops on the west face, and in some areas the rotten rock leads to adrenaline-pumping excitement. And, perhaps with the exception of Antarctica, the birdlife is like nothing I've seen on Earth."

Recreational climbing was banned on the spire in 1982 when the Lord Howe Island Act was amended, but in 1990 this was changed, and some climbing is now allowed, subject to strict conditions.

An imposing sight from any angle, Balls Pyramid has inspired and challenged adventurers keen to climb its steep faces. AUSTRALIAN GEOGRAPHIC founder Dick Smith officially claimed the 551 m spire for Australia "for a bit of fun" during his 1979 climb. "One of the best parts is that you have to swim on to the pyramid," says Dick. "You grab hold of a ledge as the waves drop away, and then swing yourself up."

night skinks can be found running on the ground and geckos may be spotted scrambling along tree limbs.

One of the most visible signs of human impact on Blackburn are Norfolk Island pines. Planted there in the days before aircraft flew to Lord Howe, they're now trimmed regularly for safety reasons. A less-attractive reminder of the past is the concrete tank on the north-eastern shore – a remnant of a small 1930s sharking industry that caught and processed grey whaler or reef sharks, which abound in the waters around Lord Howe. The industry lasted less than a year – the mainland entrepreneur who started it disappeared and the plant was abandoned.

A slightly larger islet, Mutton Bird Island, sits 1.3 km east of Mutton Bird Point and is clearly visible from Transit Hill, Blinky Beach, Boat Harbour and The Clear Place. Pyramid-shaped, it rises from a rock platform, reaching 73 m in height. On calm days it's possible for boats to land on its north-western side, enabling visitors to reach the grassy summit via a natural rock stairway on the south-eastern face. Wedge-tailed and little shearwaters dig their burrows in shallow soil on the western slope among the coarse native grass *Cyperus lucidus*. Also visible from Boat Harbour is Sail Rock, an impressive 17 m high stack just to the west of Mutton Bird Island. Masked boobies roost in the grasses growing on its small, flat summit.

Just off Lord Howe's southernmost tip, beneath the towering ramparts of Mount Gower, lies flat-topped Gower Island, home to sooty terns and masked boobies. Landings are rarely attempted here, but a good view of the 2 ha islet rewards tour-boat passengers who travel through the narrow passage separating Gower from the main island.

MISSING TREASURE

The whaler *George*, which ran aground east of Mt Gower in December 1830, was carrying a chest of gold and coins. When they'd made it ashore to a small rocky cove now called Georges Bay, the crew hid the chest. Fearing unfriendly natives, they remained there for several weeks before being picked up by the brig *Mary Elizabeth* and whaler *Nelson*. A year later the ship *Caroline* visited in search of the treasure, but it wasn't found then and hasn't been discovered since.

Nooks and knobs, underwater caves and other interesting terrain abound around the offshore islets. It's ideal diving territory and varied habitat for many sea creatures, including trevally (opposite). Appearing silvery-white from below and greenish-blue from above, these speedy fish sometimes grow to nearly 1 m long. Divers and anglers aren't the only ones whose sport brings them to appreciate Lord Howe waters. After hundreds of kilometres of open ocean, yachties crossing the Tasman Sea gratefully moor at semi-sheltered anchorages (left) within The Lagoon, from where they set off to explore the Admiraltys (above) and the other offshore islands. However, permission must be sought from the LHI Board before landing on any of the islets.

Island life

by Chris Murray

Without a care in the world, 18-month-old Brooke Busteed – one of Lord Howe's youngest residents – is thrown high above The Lagoon's clean water by her dad Peter. Like the 330 or so other island residents, Peter adores the relaxed lifestyle. "Lord Howe has a safe, clean environment for children, and I love being close to the water for swimming and snorkelling – something I can share with my family."

A hushed group of about 100 people stands on the grass outside Lord Howe Island's cluttered and aged museum. The distant sound of surf is carried on the sou'-westerly breeze, but lofty Norfolk Island pines form a screen around the scene so the air feels still and balmy, redolent with the aromas of the sea and freshly baked cakes and biscuits. My gaze drifts from the stunning backdrop, glimpsed through the pines, of Mt Lidgbird and Mt Gower, to the focus of our gathering – an Australian flag draped over a waist-high cairn of black volcanic rock.

It's 17 February 1998, the 210th anniversary of the island's discovery. Each year, Discovery Day is a time for the dedication of new endeavours, and today the cairn – to be unveiled by NSW Minister for the Environment, Pam Allan – marks the beginning of a project to raise funds for a new museum building. About 10,000 tourists visit Lord Howe each year, and the building will provide them with a showcase of the island's natural attributes.

Nearly all functions on Lord Howe attract official guests and a cross-section of residents, and today's is no exception. I can see the State politician representing Lord Howe, along with some of his predecessors, and solo-round-the-world yachties Kay Cottee and Ian Kiernan, who is best known these days as chairman of Clean Up Australia. Locals include Harry Woolnough, museum patron and, at 93 years of age, Lord Howe's oldest resident, to 37 fresh-faced children from the primary school who sing the national anthem and their school song.

Nurturing native plants

Among the guests at today's ceremony is Larry Wilson, manager of the island nursery, who has supplied the decorations – a wonderful array of potted palms and other native plants – for the occasion. In fact my day had started shortly after 7 a.m. with a visit to the nursery to pick up the plants and deliver them to the museum. In the nursery's 24 greenhouses, the island's four endemic palms are raised for export, chief among them the kentia palm – arguably the world's most attractive palm. Each year, between 2 and 3 million seedlings are carefully nurtured by a staff of five permanent workers and up to 10 casuals and then exported from Lord Howe to markets in the Netherlands, Spain, the USA, Korea and Japan.

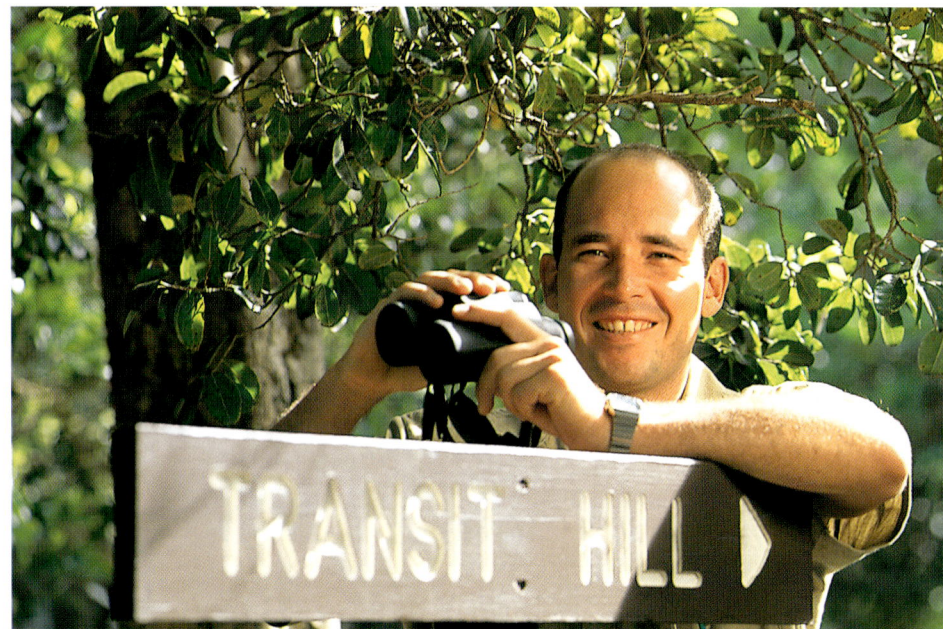

"Money from the sale of nursery products is the major source of revenue for the island Administration," Larry had told me that morning. "Not only is the money returned to the community in the form of local-government works, it also provides income for the contract workers who collect the seed, and the people employed full- and part-time here at the nursery."

And it's the nursery that has spearheaded the reafforestation effort on the island by growing native seedlings and supplying them free of charge to island residents. Foreshore, road verges and some cow pastures are slowly being returned to native forest with the assistance of the Board rangers, a small Landcare group and other enthusiastic islanders, many of whom are also replanting their household gardens.

Fishing, freight and fun

After dropping the plants off at the museum, I'd gone to Signal Point where, as part of the reafforestation effort, I'm planting melaleuca, bully bush and wedding lilies around a wooden bench-seat on the foreshore. The bench commands a magnificent view of the place where the Catalina and Sandringham flying-boats that brought visitors to the island moored, and is intended as a reminder of that era, the years from 1947 to 1974. The seat also overlooks the jetty where the coastal trading vessels *Sitka* and *Island Trader* tie up during their fortnightly calls to unload a grab bag of cargo taken aboard in the Clarence River near Yamba, in northern NSW.

PHOTOS: GRAHAME McCONNELL

When the ships arrive, on a turnabout roster, the jetty comes to life as trucks, fork-lifts and workers race around getting foodstuffs, fuel, gas, building materials, road ballast and vehicles ashore. They also load a small amount of outbound freight, which often includes glass and aluminium cans bound for the recyclers.

With no ship in, the scene that morning was relatively tranquil. A small group watched as the island tour boat *Belle Chase* nosed into the jetty to pick up passengers for a two-hour round-the-island cruise. The *Belle Chase* is also one of four vessels that fish for tuna and kingfish, their catch – often hundreds of kilos – going to the Sydney Fish Market. As freight and handling agent for Eastern Australia and Sunstate airlines, I needed to ask skipper Gary Payten the size and weight of today's fish consignment.

You could say Gary has fish oil in his blood. "My grandfather Toge Payten and a business partner, Phil Dignam, were among the first islanders to start exporting fish," he told me as we strolled along the jetty. "Phil installed the first freezer on Lord Howe in 1936, enabling them to freeze and store the catch."

The island community

After waving Gary and his passengers off, I headed towards the small village centre, which comprises the post office, public hall, power station, an airline office, two shops, a tiny office where the island newspaper is produced, and the visitor

Working together. With a spirit typical of small communities, islanders usually have several jobs, often adding agriculture, tourism and fishing to their other work. President and curator of the LHI Museum Jim Dorman (opposite below), pictured with a WWII radar, retails palm seedlings, offers guided walks and opens his home, HERITAGE HOUSE, for visitors. In the forests, Chris Haseldon (opposite above left) vigilantly fills rat-poison stations for the LHI Board environmental section, which is headed by ranger Dean Hiscox (opposite right). Dean's responsibilities include protection of the marine environment – something fishing-boat operator and manager of BEACHCOMBER LODGE Gary Payten (above left), depends on. "There's a constant demand for fresh fish at the local lodges and restaurants, as well as a mainland market," Gary says. Meanwhile, production of the island's biggest export – kentia palms – is carefully documented by nursery manager Larry Wilson and assistant Annette Thompson (above).

Nestled below Mt Lidgbird and Intermediate Hill, the island's nine-hole golf course (above), with its views across The Lagoon, must be among the most picturesque in the world. Vivienne Crombie (opposite above left, back to camera) prefers fishing to golf when she's not serving customers at Thompson's Store – one of two general stores that stock everything from fishing tackle to food. The small "urban" area and relaxed lifestyle means that bicycles are the preferred mode of transport for islanders of all ages – including school pupils Courteny Turner and Jessica Vaughan (opposite right), and Gai Wilson (opposite below left), frequent winner of the slow bicycle race at the Discovery Day games night.

GRAHAME McCONNELL

GRAHAME McCONNELL

centre. An air-communications and flight-service office during the flying-boat era, the visitor centre is opened on weekdays from 9 a.m. to 12.30 p.m. Manager Sandy Beaumont gives visitors advice about the island's natural attractions and facilities and the guided walks, tours and boat trips available.

Sandy was the founding secretary of the LHI Preservation Movement, the island's first conservation group which was founded in 1977, and she's thrilled by the progress made in recent years to solve problems associated with waste-water management and garbage disposal.

"It's been a long, hard struggle to make the environment a key priority," she told me. "Islanders – who've been here for generations – are understandably wary of any outside interference. They feel they've done a reasonable job of keeping the ecology intact, and Lord Howe is certainly in better shape than many other small oceanic islands.

"However, we've had to accept outside input in the form of technical advice, funding and ecologically sound regulations, and the community is at last starting to support initiatives which could push Lord Howe to the forefront as a model of environmental management."

As we chatted, Sandy's father Jim Whistler arrived with some notes for the next edition of the *Signal*, Lord Howe's fortnightly newspaper. When compared with the big-city newspapers, the *Signal* is the publishing equivalent of a patch-work quilt: as well as local news, it contains clippings from other newspapers, community notices, history-trivia questions, letters to the editor, advertisements, sports notices, tides, weather statistics, and Jim's impressions of the changing scene at Lord Howe. He's been editing the publication on a voluntary basis since 1954.

I then headed for the post office where, as freight agent, I had to collect the outbound mail. Postmistress Vicki Green and her assistant Darrin Nobbs were weighing mail for the daily flight to Sydney. Like many island residents, Vicki has more than one economic string to her bow: she and her husband John also run the Top Shop, which sells fresh food and groceries – and fuel from the island's only bowser. She also represents a package-holiday company and Kentialink, who provide air services between Lord Howe, Port Macquarie, Coffs Harbour and Norfolk Island.

From the post office, I wandered up to Thompson's Store where I was greeted by the irresistible aroma of freshly baked bread and pastries. Proprietors Vivienne and Gary Crombie run the island's only bakery, producing a variety of breads and pastries every day but Saturday. Theirs is the archetypal one-stop corner shop into which everything is crammed: bread, groceries, frozen goods, videos, hardware, gardening tools, takeaway foods and an exceptional array of fishing gear. Gary also operates three fishing-charter vessels and sits with eight other islanders on the Marine Advisory Committee, which advises the LHI Board on marine protection.

"Any commercial or recreational angler with any sense realises that successful fishing relies on the availability of good fish stocks, as well as a healthy marine

PHOTOS: GRAHAME McCONNELL

*Friendly fishing rivals for 40 years, T-shirt-clad Brian Simpson and Jim Whistler (above)
examine a squid stranded on Lagoon Beach after a night of light westerlies and falling
tide. The two often make early-morning forays for fishing bait, as does Jack Shick (right),
who sometimes lends a hand on island fishing vessels. Many islanders own a boat,
and one of the oldest is VIKING, lovingly maintained by Donald Payten (opposite below).
Built in Sydney in 1935, the 10 m wooden vessel was motored to Lord Howe in 1952.
Brian Busteed (opposite top) has far more modern technology aboard his boat BLUE
GROPER. Operator of Howea Divers, Brian introduces about 100 people each year to
the adventurous sport of scuba diving.*

GRAHAME McCONNELL

Up before the dawn chorus of birds, Jamie Elliott (above) mixes and weighs the dough for a range of breads, pastries and cakes at Lord Howe's only bakery. It's a job that gives him the afternoons off for pursuing his other interests – like fishing. Another early riser, fourth-generation islander Barry Thompson (opposite below), plucks figs on his half-hectare property before breakfast. Many locals grow some of their own produce – Barry's crops include corn, pumpkins, tomatoes and spinach – but most fruit and vegetables come by ship or, like the mail, by plane. Darrin Nobbs and Vicki Green dish out the parcels and letters from the tiny post office in Neds Beach Rd (opposite above). As there's no household delivery, the office becomes a popular social meeting place on mail-plane days.

environment," Gary told me. "Dedication of marine reserves is vital for the preservation of marine life, just as many animal species have been saved from extinction by land-based parks and reserves."

After buying some fresh rolls and pastries, I drove back along Lagoon Road, where I picked up a beaming Tom and Elaine Price, residents of Brisbane who've been visiting Lord Howe for a much-enjoyed holiday every year since 1976. They were on their way to join a glass-bottomed boat for a trip to North Bay, one of the island's loveliest, secluded beaches, and I dropped them at their departure point near Blue Peter Cafe where boat operator Peter Busteed was busy loading gear. Half a dozen local tour operators such as Peter help visitors make the most of their stay, organising boat trips and popular guided walks, including the spectacular climb up Mt Gower.

Airways – a vital link

With the morning nearly gone, it was home for a quick lunch before donning my airline-agent uniform and heading to the airport for the afternoon flights from and to Sydney. Lodge proprietors soon arrived with departing guests, keeping me and my two assistants busy as we checked in a full complement of 32 passengers. In the brief interval between the plane's arrival and departure, lodge owners and I chatted about fishing, golf scores, the weather and snippets of island gossip.

There are 17 guesthouses on the island, ranging in size from *Pinetrees*, with 85 beds, down to *Mary Challis* and *Waimarie*, which have four each. Many of the lodges are on land that's been held by the same family for generations. Judy Riddle, proprietor of *Leanda Lei* guesthouse, reflected on her clientele: "Most of our visitors come here specifically to avoid the high-rises, shopping malls and night-clubs typical of most resort towns. They love the fact that it's peaceful and unspoilt, and we know they get a favourable impression because we have a substantial amount of repeat business, with some families and couples coming year after year, and others more than once."

Our conversation was interrupted by the arrival of the Eastern Australia Airlines Dash 8 aircraft. While the passengers disembarked I unloaded freight and luggage and was soon joined by the always-cheerful Gower Wilson, who began refuelling the plane. Gower sits on the island Board and is also its "Mr Fixit", responsible for the repair and maintenance of an extraordinary array of Board equipment, from the humble sludge pump and lawnmower to a crane, the Caterpillar bulldozer and the diesel generators at the powerhouse. He's also an out-standing seaman.

Wearing one of his many official hats, Gower represents the inspection branch of the NSW Roads and Traffic Authority, and is responsible for certifying the road-worthiness of the 289 vehicles registered on the island. He remembers the days during and immediately after WWII when the island Administration tried to prohibit privately owned vehicles. The ban didn't last and the vehicle population has bur-geoned ever since. "The Board is now looking at all possibilities to control vehicle numbers which, it's generally agreed, are too high," Gower said.

With passengers and luggage aboard and refuelling completed, the Dash 8 tax-ied out and took to the air, leaving me with some freight to deliver.

Two special places

The first item I had to deliver was a consignment for the golf club, only a stone's throw from the airport and blessed by dramatic surroundings: mounts Gower and Lidgbird on one side and the island lagoon on the other.

At the clubhouse I ran into Tony Cameron, energetic volunteer organiser for the club. He's developing a long-term plan to make Lord Howe Island's nine-hole course one of the best of its kind in Australia. "I reckon we already have the most picturesque golf course in the world," said Tony. "But we're particularly conscious of the need to landscape with native trees, along with the reshaping of the fairways and greens."

My second delivery was to ex-serviceman and one-time miner Esven Fenton, who I found checking his small herd of 20 cows on the 12-hectare special lease he holds. I asked whether he lamented the passing of the island's self-sufficient econ-omy, which had survived into the 1950s. "It was inevitable that the island would

PHOTOS: GRAHAME McCONNELL

Painting the grass with mauve blooms, a jacaranda – one of only two on the island – frames BEACHCOMBER LODGE (below) on Anderson Road, a guesthouse licensed for 15 visitors. Built in 1913 as a private residence, the lodge has since been extended, but still retains its early island character, as do many of the 17 guesthouses. Also in Anderson Rd, MANDALAY (right) – a private home previously called PALM HAVEN – was built about 1920 for William Whiting, who married local girl Sue Nichols. Their descendants – who run a guesthouse in the same road that's now called PALM HAVEN – named the popular island restaurant Aunty Sue's after her.

GRAHAME McCONNELL

PHOTOS: GRAHAME McCONNELL

Built to suit the mild climate and easygoing lifestyle, most island homes have wide verandas that encourage outdoor living. Many homes like KENTIA *(above, left and right) are also surrounded by dense foliage, not so much for privacy, but to help protect against the winter winds. The house was built in 1905 from a Hudson kit home for Alex Fenton, who came to the island to collect palm seed and plants for Searles seed company. Collecting something quite different in their bucket, residents Margaret Murray (left, at left) and Jane O'Leary share a laugh over their self-designed mouse trap. Introduced mice, increasingly becoming a pest on the island, are lured down a rope into the bucket towards plentiful food supplies that they can't reach without jumping off the rope. Once in the bucket, they can't scale the sides or reach the rope.*

PHOTOS: GRAHAME McCONNELL

become less self-sufficient as it was steadily integrated with the mainland economy and we all became more affluent through tourism," he said. "However, I still think the local running of cattle is worthwhile, and a good use of my special lease."

Conserving a unique environment

Back at the museum for the official ceremony I found Jim Dorman leading the island contingent and officiating at the function. Jim, voluntary museum curator and the driving force behind the new building, arrived on Lord Howe about 40 years ago and developed a passion for collecting memorabilia – old bottles, photographs, medallions, documents and a host of intriguing items found mouldering away in island sheds, storerooms and closets or thrown out on the island tip.

I take a few moments to chat with Greg Leaman, the Lord Howe Island Board's manager whose job it is to oversee almost every government activity on the island. His responsibilities include administration of land tenure, parks management, the hospital, power generation, roads, the airstrip and maintenance of public works – even acting as a marriage celebrant or funeral director when the occasion demands.

"The manager's role is largely one of balancing protection of the island's unique environment against those community needs which might compete or even conflict," Greg says. "Fortunately, the strong conservation ethic and sense of local pride among island residents help ensure that a sensible and workable balance is maintained."

KEEP OFF DUNE

I first came to live on Lord Howe in 1959, and in recent years I've been delighted to see this greater appreciation of the environment, with many residents actively protecting their unique asset. From the conservation of marine resources to promoting the use of renewable energy, management of solid waste and household waste water, the community seems to have reached some consensus on undoing past damage and protecting nature's bounty. Not everyone is convinced of the importance of these issues, but recent community surveys have shown that up to 70 per cent of islanders want to improve the track record on waste management and related problems, even if some extra expense might be incurred. With this level of support, Lord Howe may become an environmental model for other small communities to follow.

With Greg is ranger Dean Hiscox. Since the island was added to the World Heritage list in 1982, Board rangers have played an increasingly important part in the care and maintenance of the environment: building walking tracks, providing interpretive signs and information, and controlling noxious weeds and feral animals. Like many other locals, Dean believes the new museum will greatly benefit visitors and enrich their stay.

"Many things about the island are unique – the Lord Howe woodhen for example. The museum will give us the opportunity to show off some of these things, especially those that aren't so well known, with photos, displays and audiovisual presentations."

Lining up for the final approach to the island, Eastern Australia Airlines pilots (opposite above) prepare to land their 36-seater, turbo-prop Boeing Dash 8 after a two-hour flight from Sydney. Nestled between The Lagoon and Blinky Beach at the foot of the mountains, the 900 m long airstrip (opposite below) – which has strong prevailing westerlies in winter and only a handful of calm days each year – demands great concentration, even from experienced pilots.

After a 40-hour journey from the Clarence River on the NSW north coast, the 500-tonne ISLAND TRADER off-loads 200-litre drums of diesel, aviation fuel and petrol (below). Lord Howe's community is still reliant on shipping for most large commodities, and the vessel's 2.5 m draught enables it to dock at the jetty. It's a costly way to deliver fuel, so the price per litre at the island's only bowser (below left) is nearly double the amount paid by vehicle owners in Sydney.

GRAHAME McCONNELL

GRAHAME McCONNELL

Celebrating Discovery Day

I make my final freight delivery of the day at the Lord Howe Bowling Club. The club is the main watering hole for locals and on most afternoons a convivial crowd gathers there. Lawn bowls has been played on the island since 1922 and games are still played every Thursday afternoon.

Work over, I meet my wife Margaret and our daughter Zoe at Lagoon Beach for a swim. Peter Busteed, his trip to North Bay completed, is also there enjoying a dip. The tide has turned and the water reaches higher up the lagoon shore.

A few hours later, and we're off to the cricket ground to enjoy the Discovery Day Sports night, the one night of the year when nearly all islanders are out and about. In the grounds of the adjacent school trestle tables are set up, huge bowls of salad appear and the aroma of deep-fried kingfish-and-chips draws a crowd. Zoe bounces excitedly around with the other children, waiting for the games to start.

Discovery Day Sports has been a feature of island life since Jim Whistler organised the first such event in 1954. As well as standard track races, there's a palm-climbing competition, a 200-litre-drum-rolling race, a slow bicycle race (last over the line wins) and a three-legged race. Everyone has a great time until the night winds up at about 10 p.m.

The island today

In the past couple of years some changes have taken place on the island. For museum curator Jim Dorman the dream and years of hard work have come to fruition and the new museum is open, with the island visitor centre relocated there.

The Post Office is now run by Peter Philipps, the island's aviation buff and author of a book on aviation of LHI. The LHI Board has a new manager, Murray Carter, who has a strong interest in conservation and is dedicated to balancing the needs of the community with the environment.

Some major environmental initiatives have been taken – waste recycling and a vertical composting unit have been installed; a wind-powered electricity generator is planned. A bulk food cooperative is now running, as part of the effort to decrease packaging, and hence waste, on the island. Surrounding the island and Balls Pyramid is a State Marine Park out to three nautical miles and a Commonwealth Marine Park from 3 to 10 nautical miles, with a full-time marine park manager on the island. There have been big increases in funding for environmental projects and a new era of conservation is emerging.

Despite these changes the island's tranquillity and lifestyle are still the same. Lord Howe Island is increasing its profile as one of the best nature-based and ecologically sustainable destinations in the world.

Chris Murray is honorary secretary and archivist of the Lord Howe Island museum.

GRAHAME McCONNELL

On one of the rare summer days on which the summits of mounts Gower and Lidgbird are free of cloud, White Gallinule's cane chairs (opposite) bask in the glow of the late-afternoon sun. The restaurant, at CAPELLA LODGE near Lovers Bay, is one of 12 on the island offering a wide range of fine cuisine. Another popular spot where locals and tourists mingle for a coffee or a meal is Blue Peter Cafe (above), whose kitchen is stocked with some locally grown produce.

Lord Howe Island lies off the NSW central coast, 550 km due east of Port Macquarie and approximately 700 km north-east of Sydney. Pre-trip information is available from the Lord Howe Visitor Centre, ☎ (02) 6563 2114.

Getting there

Qantaslink operates approximately eight return flights out of Sydney each week and out of Brisbane one flight on Sundays only. Qantaslink operates 36-seater Dash 8 aircraft on the route and the flight takes about two hours each way.
Enquiries/bookings ☎ 13 13 13.

There are moorings in the lagoon for visiting vessels. For information ☎ (02) 6563 2266; or write to: The Port Operations Manager, PO Box 28, Lord Howe Island, NSW 2898; or via radio: Lord Howe Maritime HF 4125, also VHF channel 12 or 16.

Island service levy

There's a $20 fee included in the price of a plane ticket. This goes towards maintenance of facilities such as barbecues, picnic areas, walking tracks, water tanks, etc.

Accommodation

There are 17 family-run guesthouses on the island, ranging in size from 4 guest beds to 85. Types of accommodation include: guesthouse with all meals provided; self-contained with full kitchen facilities; self-contained with breakfast-making facilities only. Bed and breakfast packages are also available.

Camping is not permitted on the island.

Climate

Average summer temperatures from 19°C to 25°C; winter 13°C–18°C. Frosts are unknown. Most rain falls during winter. Water temperatures range from 17°C in winter to 25°C in late summer. Best swimming December–April.

When to go

For nature enthusiasts, seabirds are most active September–March; peak plant-flowering time is November–January. Winter is generally windy, cooler and wetter, but great for bushwalking. The recommended minimum stay is one week.

What to bring

Good walking shoes, sunscreen, hat, light windcheater, torch, waterbottle. Dress at restaurants is smart casual. Island shops carry a range of clothes and pharmacy items. Photographers should bring spare batteries and slide film. Pack carefully: there's a 15 kg weight limit on aircraft.

Getting around

One of the delights of a LHI holiday is that you don't need a car: cycling and walking are the main forms of transport. Some lodges hire out bicycles, otherwise try Wilson's Hire Service ☎ (02) 6563 2045. A few hire cars are available (speed limit 25 km/h), from Wilson's, Leanda Lei ☎ (02) 6563 2195 and Thompson's Store ☎ (02) 6563 2155. Most lodges bus guests to restaurants at night.

Dining out

The island has 12 restaurants, 10 fully licensed. A couple are home-style kitchens open limited hours. It's advisable to make dinner bookings before noon. Gary and Vivienne Crombie bake fresh bread and pastries daily, available at Thompson's Store. Some shops and restaurants sell takeaway food. If you're planning a picnic shops carry a wide range of food items; there are a number of barbecues available for use at scenic beach locations.

Activities

The island offers many outdoor activities: walking, swimming, reef-walking, beachcombing, snorkelling, surfing, fishing, birdwatching and photography.

For information on guided walks, fishing charters and bus and boat trips, watch the noticeboards at your guesthouse or the Visitor Centre. Bookings essential.

The glass-bottomed vessels Coral Princess and Coral Empress operate snorkelling and coral-viewing trips daily, except Saturday, weather and tides permitting. Islander Cruises operate snorkelling trips to North Bay and at the southern end of the Lagoon through the week. Two boats – Phasmid and Kermadec – run sightseeing and birding trips to Balls Pyramid when weather allows.

The island's two scuba-diving operators offer dive charters and courses: Prodive Travel ☎ (02) 9232 5733; Howea Divers ☎ (02) 6563 2290. Snorkelling equipment can be hired from Wilson's Hire Service, Thompson's Store and at Neds Beach; several guesthouses have their own snorkelling gear.

If you're planning to have a boat trip during your holiday, it's advisable to go on the first calm day – don't delay. Note that there are no motorboats for hire on LHI.

Island Museum

The Island Museum is open six days a week, Sunday to Friday, 9.00 a.m to 4.00 p.m. Within the Museum is the Coral Cafe, open for coffee and light lunches. Books and local art and craft are on sale. Natural history talks by local experts are held most afternoons.
☎ (02) 6563 2111.

Sports

Tennis: *Blue Lagoon* has courts and raquets for general hire (bookings at Thompson's Store). Pinetrees and Oceanview have tennis courts and raquets for their own guests only.

Bowls: Visitors are welcome to play in the chicken run commencing 4.00 p.m. Thursdays at Lord Howe Bowling Club. Casual dress acceptable; bowls shoes mandatory.
☎ (02) 6563 2171.

Golf: Visitors welcome every day at the 9-hole course but it's reserved for competition on Fridays from 3.00 p.m. and Sundays from 1.00 p.m. – visitors are welcome to compete. Hire clubs available on an honour system.
☎ (02) 6563 2179.

Banks and credit cards

There's a Commonwealth Bank (next to the LHI Board office) and a Westpac agency (next toThompson's Store). There are no ATMs on the island and EFTPOS facilities are limited. Visa, MasterCard and Bankcard are accepted widely.

Medical and pharmaceutical

The hospital's clinic and dispensary are open weekdays from 8.30 a.m.–12.30 p.m. At other times the doctor may be contacted by phone.

Holiday bookings

Airfare/accommodation packages are the best value for LHI visitors. Your local travel agent can arrange these, or book through wholesaler travel agents. See theLord Howe Island website www.lordhoweisland.info for details.

For an escorted eight-day nature tour with the author, contact Ian Hutton at PO Box 157 Lord Howe Island 2898. Email lhitours@tpgi.com.au.

Inviting walkers over the fence, a simple stile suggests a stroll through verdant grass down to The Lagoon's treasure-filled water. The whole island is ideal for exploring and offers something for all – from relaxing meanders along sunny beaches before a morning coffee, to heart-thumping climbs up mountains. And with only 393 tourists allowed at any one time, Lord Howe's sparkling solitude can be experienced by all who visit.

GRAHAME McCONNELL

Family Arecaceae

Big mountain palm
Hedyscepe canterburyana

Endemic compact palm growing from altitude of 350 m to mountain summits. Grey trunk to 10 m high, 20 cm thick; prominent rings 2–5 cm apart. **Leaves:** Dark green, 2–3 m long; blue-grey bases form 50 cm sheaths on upper trunk. **Flowers:** March–August; yellow, on 30–40 cm long, many-branched stems that grow below blue sheath. **Fruit:** Egg-shaped, about 5 cm long; dull red when ripe.

Curly palm
Howea belmoreana

Common endemic palm found on sloping sites with basalt soils up to about 400 m. Trunk to 12 m, 15 cm thick, ringed by leaf scars. **Leaves:** Individual leaf spikes (leaflets) curl up off midrib. Strongly arched leaves 3–5 m long. **Flowers:** November–

December; creamy brown, arranged spirally on spikes arising from the bases of the lower leaves. **Fruit:** Lemon-shaped, 3–4 cm long; ripening to brown or red.

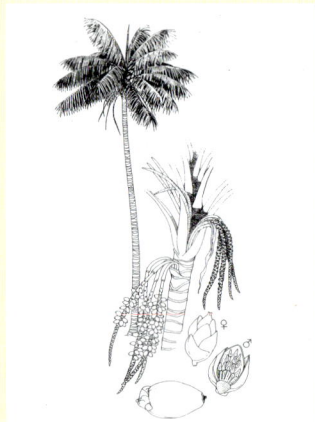

Kentia or thatch palm
Howea forsteriana

Tall endemic palm, widespread on lowlands, preferring flat sites

with calcarenite soils. Trunk to 15 m high, 15 cm thick. **Leaves:** Leaflets drop down off the midrib. Leaves 3–5 m long, the stalk drooping slightly. **Flowers:** August–October; usually 3–5 flower spikes 1 m long, fused at the base into a short, flattened stalk; flowers and fruit similar to those of *H. belmoreana*.

Little mountain or moorei palm
Lepidorrhachis mooreana

A stout endemic dwarf palm restricted to mountain tops. Trunk rarely more than 2 m high, 15 cm thick; prominently scarred with rings 1–2 cm apart. **Leaves:** Arching, 1.5 m long; swollen bases form a deep-green sheath on upper trunk. **Flowers:** August–December; cream on a multi-branched stem. **Fruit:** Marble-sized, red.

Family Flagellariaceae

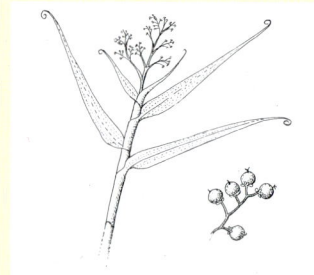

Bush cane
Flagellaria indica

Robust climber to 10 m or more. Straight, cane-like stem, 1 cm thick. **Leaves:** Narrow, 10–30 cm long, alternate, tapering at both ends, tip forming a coiled tendril. **Flowers:** August–February; numerous, in clusters; cream, 2 mm across. **Fruit:** Reddish-brown, round, about 5 mm wide.

Family Iridaceae

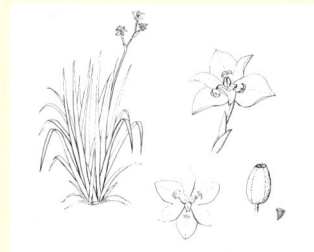

Wedding lily
Dietes robinsoniana

Perennial, endemic herb to 1.5 m high; common in open sites in mountains, e.g. Far Flats and Goat House Cave. Creeping underground stem. **Leaves:** Blue-green, straplike, 1 m long. **Flowers:** July–November; three-petalled, white with yellow

markings on much-branched, long stalk. Each flower, 9 cm across, opens for one day only. **Fruit:** Cylindrical capsule 4 x 2.5 cm; green, drying to brown.

Family Orchidaceae

Bulbophyllum argyropus

A small epiphyte growing on trees or rocks. Creeping root structure often forms dense mat. **Leaves:** Oblong-linear, 20–30 x 5 mm; whitish sheath at base, into swollen part of stem. **Flowers:** August–September; white or cream, 7 mm long; 2–4 on short stalk. **Fruit:** A ribbed capsule 6 mm long.

Calanthe triplicata

Rare ground-growing orchid found at Erskine Valley,

Mt Gower and Dinner Run. **Leaves:** 4–10 ragged-ended, usually narrow-obovate leaves, each 20–50 x 4–8 cm; arise from conical swollen stem part. **Flowers:** November–March; numerous, white, 30 mm across; on top of stem to 1 m high. **Fruit:** 3–4 cm long capsule.

Corybas barbarae

A 2 cm high ground-hugging herb; only one colony known on LHI, on Malabar–Kims Lookout Ridge. **Leaves:** Single, heart-shaped leaf, 1.5–3 x 2–3.5 cm; absent September–March when plant is dormant as a small underground tuber. **Flowers:** May–June, 15 x 9 mm, whitish with purple streaks; appearing on short stalk that elongates to 12 cm after fertilisation.

Bush orchid
Dendrobium macropus
subsp. *howeanum*

Endemic epiphyte; large clumps common in lowland forests and up to about 450 m. Stems stand erect. **Leaves:** Stiff, about 13 x 2.5 cm; usually 3–6 at the end of cane-like stem. **Flowers:** September–November; 14 mm long, dull yellow; lowest petal

cream with purple blotches. 5–20 clustered along stalk to 10 cm long. **Fruit:** 25 x 14 mm capsule, green with purple dots and purple blotched ribs.

Moorei orchid
Dendrobium moorei

Endemic epiphyte on tree branches, occasionally on rocks and cliffs. Common in the southern mountains from about 400 m to summits. Erect stems. **Leaves:** 6–12 x 2 cm, dark green, leathery; usually 4–5 crowded at end of furrowed cylindrical stem up to 20 cm long. **Flowers:** All year, peaking December–May; white, 18 mm long, drooping, some with pink blotches inside; 5–15

clustered along thin stalk to 8 cm long. **Fruit:** 20 mm long, green capsule.

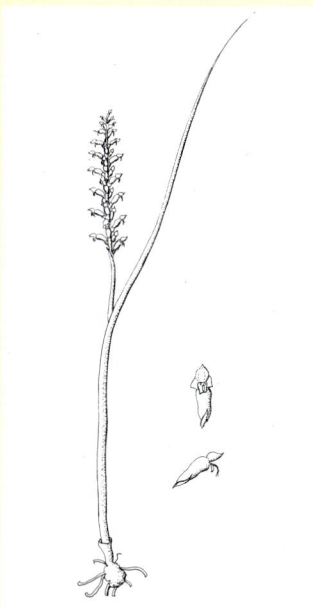

Microtis unifolia

Slender herb, 10–40 cm high. Found in small colonies in northern hills; exists as underground tuber for part of year. **Leaves:** Single, 8–60 cm long, cylindrical. **Flowers:** October–January; numerous, 12 mm long, green or yellow-green, spiralled around spike. **Fruit:** 5 mm long ribbed capsule.

Plectorrhiza erecta

Endemic epiphyte found low down on trees and shrubs, occasionally on cliffs. Erect, wiry stem to 30 cm long, supported by thick white roots emanating below

leaves. Many plants form a tangled mass. **Leaves:** 30 x 10 mm, tapering at both ends; light green, fleshy. **Flowers:** November–December; 4 mm long, yellow–orange, with profuse, small purple blotches on inside surfaces; lowest petal large, cream and winged. About six flowers line each 25 mm long stalk.

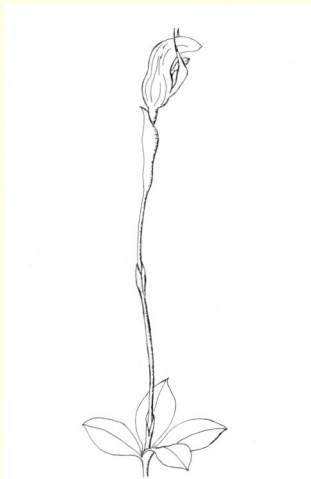

Pterostylis curta

Slender herb, rare on LHI. Erect stem 10–30 cm tall. **Leaves:** 2–6, 1.5–10 x 1–3 cm, broadly elliptical, arranged in circle around

stem's base. **Flowers:** July–October; solitary, about 2 cm long; green, shaded with red. **Fruit:** 15 mm long capsule, drying to split longitudinally.

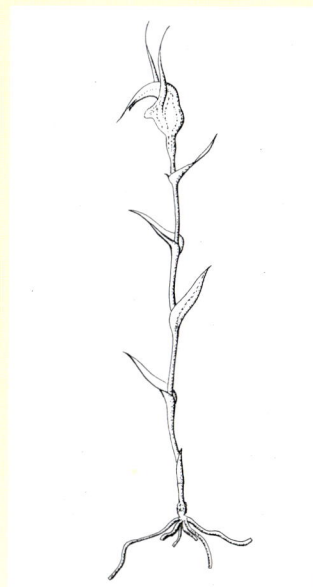

Pterostylis obtusa

Slender herb with erect stem 10–20 cm high; rare on LHI. **Leaves:** When not in flower, 3–6, egg-shaped, 1–2 cm long in circle around base. When in flower, 3–5 narrow leaves clasp the stem along its length. **Flowers:** April–May; solitary, about 2 cm long; green, striped with translucent white. **Fruit:** 15 mm long capsule, drying to split longitudinally.

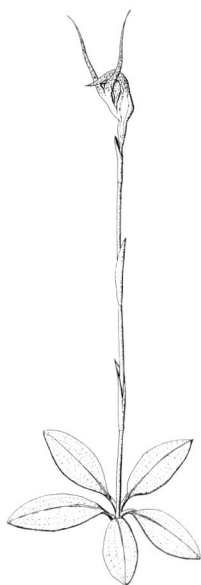

Pterostylis pedunculata

Slender herb, rare on LHI. Stem 10–25 cm high. **Leaves:** 3–6, dark-green, egg-shaped, to 3 cm long; form circle around base of stem. **Flowers:** July–October; solitary, 2 cm long; green with red-brown tips. **Fruit:** 15 mm long capsule, drying to split longitudinally.

Family Pandanaceae

Screw pine or forkedy tree
Pandanus forsteri

Endemic tree to 13 m high, common on lowlands. Prop roots 3–7 m long support tree as main stem rots. **Leaves:** Clustered at ends of branches; linear, 100–150 x 5 cm; small sharp prickles. **Flowers:** December–April; tiny female flowers covered by leaves; male flowers on 50 cm long, branched spikes, each enclosed in a white leaf. **Fruit:** Dense cluster forming a cylinder up to 20 x 15 cm. Red when ripe.

Family Philesiaceae

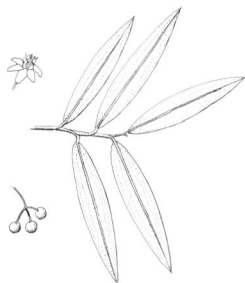

Geitonoplesium cymosum

Scrambling creeper with wiry green stem. Reasonably common in lowland forests. **Leaves:** Grass-like, alternate, light green with distinct parallel veins and prominent midvein; 8 x 1.5 cm with small hook at end. **Flowers:** November–March; white, 8 mm long; in hanging clusters. Faint, sweet perfume. **Fruit:** Purple-black berry 6–8 mm diameter.

Family Liliaceae

Swamp lily
Crinum pedunculatum

Perennial herb with thick, fleshy, erect stem up to 2 m tall. Found in many low areas close to west coast. **Leaves:** Bright green, linear, 80–150 x 15 cm; radiate in distinct tussock from stem. **Flowers:** October–January; large, white with purple stamens; in clusters at end of flattened stalk. **Fruit:** Rounded, with a point, 3 cm diameter.

Family Smilacaceae

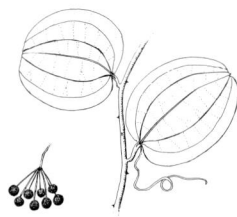

Smilax australis

Tough climber with strong prickly stem. Probably most common vine of lowland forests. **Leaves:** Alternate, broadly egg-shaped to almost round, to 10 cm diameter; five prominent longitudinal veins. **Flowers:** Spring–summer; minute, in clusters of about 20–50. **Fruit:** Clusters of shiny black, 8 mm wide berries hanging on long stalks.

Family Apocynaceae

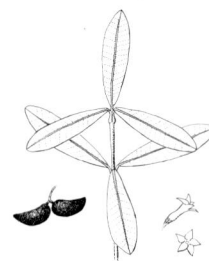

Alyxia lindii

Endemic shrub common on ridges of lowland hills; tends to climb over other trees. **Leaves:** Dark green with milky sap; oblong or egg-shaped, 6 x 2 cm; in rings of three. **Flowers:** November–February, white, 8 mm long, in clusters; five petals with twist. **Fruit:** 20 mm long; black, curved and pointed.

Christmas bush
Alyxia ruscifolia

Bush to 2 m high, widespread in understorey of lowland forests. **Leaves:** 1.5 x 1 cm, prickly; in rings of four; milky sap.

Flowers: February–August; white, 0.5 cm long; five petals with characteristic twist. Usually only 1–2 together. **Fruit:** Bright orange, 8 mm at widest; egg-shaped.

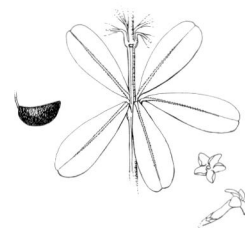

Alyxia squamulosa

Rare endemic shrub found on Mt Gower down to 700 m. Tends to climb over other trees. **Leaves:** Dark green with milky sap; 5 x 2.5 cm, rounded ends; in rings of five. **Flowers:** October–January; white, 12 mm long; five petals with a twist, in clusters to 4 cm diameter. Strongly scented, sweet but unpleasant. **Fruit:** Black, curved and pointed, 20 mm long.

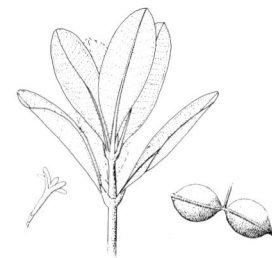

(Red) Berrywood
Ochrosia elliptica

Tree to 4 m tall, common in lowlands, especially sandy areas near coast. **Leaves:** Dark and glossy, 10 x 4.5 cm, oblong-elliptical; in rings of three. **Flowers:** November–April; white, long, narrow tube to 18 mm. **Fruit:** Ribbed, deep red, 3 cm long; present for much of year; usually paired.

Parsonsia howeana

Tall, slender-stemmed endemic climber in forest from sea level to about 700 m. **Leaves:** Opposite, 8 x 2.5 cm; light green and shiny; tapering at both ends. **Flowers:** All year; 8 mm long; orange but can vary from yellow to red; tubular with ends of petals rolled back; honey scented. **Fruit:** Hard, 10 cm long capsule, splitting open to release numerous flattened seeds.

Family Araliaceae

(Island) pine
Polyscias cissodendron

Endemic tree to 12 m, fissured bark. Reasonably common from sea level to about 400 m, mainly in sheltered forests. **Leaves:**

Compound with 11 ovate, light-green leaflets, each 7 x 4 cm and asymmetric. **Flowers:** September–November; yellow, 4 mm long, in clusters. **Fruit:** Brown, bead-like, laterally flattened; 5 x 3 mm.

Family Asclepiadaceae

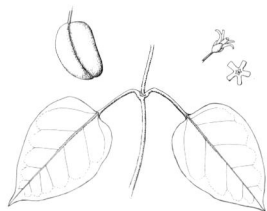

Marsdenia rostrata

Robust, twining climber common on ridges all over island. **Leaves:** Opposite, 9 x 6 cm, egg-shaped. **Flowers:** September–November; white, 12 mm across, in dense clusters. **Fruit:** Broad, brown, 7 cm long; splits into two boat-shaped halves releasing numerous small seeds with silky hairs.

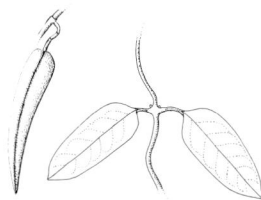

Tylophora biglandulosa

Slender climber, exudes a white latex when broken. Forms dense tangles along shore. **Leaves:** Opposite, oblong, 6 x 2.5 cm with a short point; thick and succulent, exuding copious white sap. **Flowers:** December–April; dull cream, 18 mm across, in clusters.

Fruit: Fleshy 8 cm long capsule; 2.5 cm wide at top, tapering gradually; numerous small seeds with silky hairs.

Family Asteraceae

Bully bush
Cassinia tenuifolia

Compact endemic bush to 2 m high. Common and widespread in lowlands, exposed areas and paddocks; major recoloniser of disturbed areas. **Leaves:** Alternate, crowded, linear, 2.5 x 0.1 cm; green on top, white underneath. **Flowers:** January–April; cream, 6 mm long, in groups of 5–6. Strong, sweet scent. **Fruit:** Brown, plumed, dry, 1 mm long.

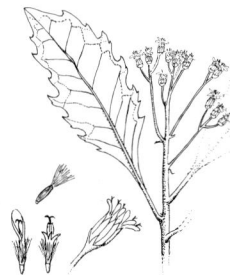

Lordhowea insularis

Erect endemic woody herb 1–2 m high. Reasonably common in moist forests from low ridges to mountain summits. **Leaves:** Alternate, deeply toothed, 8 x 4 cm. **Flowers:** May–August;

yellow, 5–7 female florets and about 16 bisexual central florets in cylindrical flowers 9 mm across. **Fruit:** Dry, plumed, thistle-like, 5 mm long.

Mountain daisy
Olearia ballii

Dense endemic shrub to 1.5 m high, found from about 400 m to summits. **Leaves:** Alternate, crowded, linear, 1.2 x 0.1 cm; upper surface dark glossy green, undersurface has fine white hairs. **Flowers:** Mainly October–February, but some all year; showy daisy head 15 mm across with white and purple florets. **Fruit:** Tiny, brown, dry; numerous bristles.

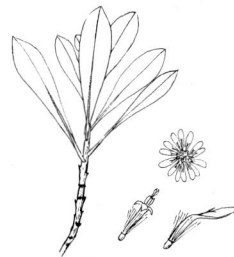

Olearia elliptica subsp. *praetermissa*

Stunted, endemic bush to 1 m, found mainly on rocky ledges of mountains at higher elevations. **Leaves:** Alternate, light green, 3 x 1 cm; sometimes sticky

underneath. Tend to cluster at ends of branches. **Flowers:** May–October; white, daisy-like, 1 cm across, with 20 white 6 mm ray florets. **Fruit:** Dry, 2 mm long; numerous bristles.

Pumpkin bush
Olearia mooneyi

Tall endemic bush or small tree, found on mountain summits from 750 m, where it's common and conspicuous. **Leaves:** Alternate, crowded, 9 x 3 cm; top surface shiny green, undersurface pale brown hairs. **Flowers:** November–January; numerous, white, daisy-like, 8 mm across. **Fruit:** Dry, brown, 6 mm long; numerous bristles.

Family Avicenniaceae

Mangrove
Avicennia marina subsp. *australasica*

Small tree to 3 m high, with spiky breathing roots. Only seven individuals, found on tidal mudflats on northern side of Hunters Bay. **Leaves:** Opposite, rhomboid-elliptical, 7 x 2.5 cm; top surface shiny green, undersurface whitish short hairs. **Flowers:** April–September; yellow-orange, 7 x 6 mm, in dense clusters. **Fruit:** Roundish leathery capsule, 30 mm long, densely covered in fine white hairs.

Family Bignoniaceae

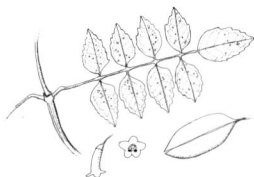

Pandorea pandorana
subsp. *austrocaledonica*

Strong woody climber growing over trees on lowland ridges to 500 m. **Leaves:** Compound, with 5–9 bright-green, toothed leaflets, each 3 x 1.5 cm. **Flowers:** August–November; 16 mm long, tubular, white with dark-red spots in throat; in loose terminal clusters; vanilla-like scent. **Fruit:** 50 mm long, flat woody capsule, numerous winged seeds inside.

Family Caesalpinia

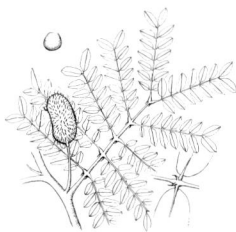

Caesalpinia bonduc

Woody scrambling shrub with sharp hooks. Only found on cliff-side at Neds Beach. **Leaves:** Alternate, to 50 cm long; five

pairs of mini-stems, each with seven pairs of oblong leaflets. **Flowers:** Late summer; bright yellow, 12–13 mm long, 20 mm in diameter, in an arrangement 12 cm long. **Fruit:** Flattish pod 8 x 4 cm, covered in dense prickles.

Family Celastraceae

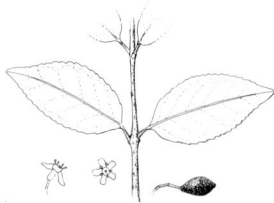

Tamana
Elaeodendron curtipendulum

Tall tree to 13 m high, common on lowland ridges. Rats gnaw its fruits, often leaving remains on walking tracks. **Leaves:** Opposite, elliptical, 6 x 3 cm; shiny and toothed. **Flowers:** May–September; minute, yellowish-green, in clusters. **Fruit:** Ovoid, 18 mm long with a short point; blue-green, ripening to almost black.

Family Chenopodiaceae

Atriplex cinerea

Hardy erect bushy shrub to 1 m tall, common on sandy sites on east coast. **Leaves:** Alternate, 6 x 1 cm, bluish-grey; oblong,

tapering at both ends. **Flowers:** October–January; tiny; males form dense, red, globular clusters in terminal spikes 5 cm long; females in small clusters or singles between leaf and stem. **Fruiting bracteoles:** 4–7 mm long.

Family Convolvulaceae

Calystegia affinis

Thin-stemmed twiner only known on LHI at bottom of Dawsons Ridge, beside Max Nicholls track. **Leaves:** Sparse, alternate, arrow-shaped, 6 x 5 cm. **Flowers:** Solitary, funnel-shaped, 3.5 cm long, pink with five cream longitudinal bands; on a thin stalk to 10 cm long. **Fruit:** unknown.

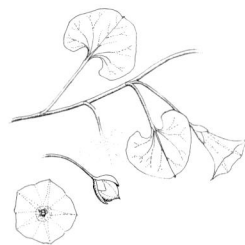

Calystegia soldenalla

Small prostrate twiner found in a few locations along beach margins and in grass to forest fringes. **Leaves:** Alternate, rounded, 4 cm across; two broad lobes at base. **Flowers:** Spring–summer; purple,

trumpet-shaped, to 4 cm long. **Fruit:** Brown capsule 1 cm across.

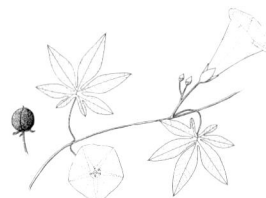

Ipomoea cairica

Common, thin-stemmed climber, found from coastal strip to lowland ridges, where it climbs small trees. **Leaves:** Alternate, to 6 cm long, divided into five or seven lobes. **Flowers:** Most of year; violet or sometimes white, trumpet-shaped, about 6 cm long. **Fruit:** A brown globular capsule, 10 mm long.

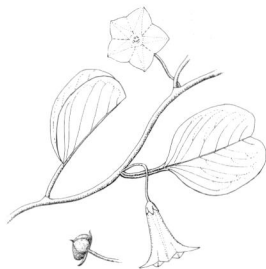

Ipomoea pes-caprae
subsp. *brasiliensis*

Trailing beach perennial with strong red trailing stem; common on edge of beaches. On Australian mainland, Aboriginal people used roots for food and boiled leaves as treatment for stings from marine animals. **Leaves:** Alternate, large, fleshy, rounded; purple stalk. **Flowers:** Summer; violet, trumpet-shaped,

about 6 cm long; open in morning and begin closing mid-afternoon. **Fruit:** A brown globular capsule 18 mm across.

Family Elaeocarpaceae

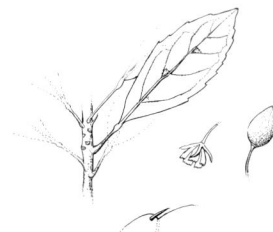

Elaeocarpus costatus

Rare endemic tree to 8 m, found from lowlands at Boat Harbour and Intermediate Hill to Mt Gower's summit. **Leaves:** Alternate, 9 x 3 cm with toothed margins, clustered towards ends of branches. Most trees have several red leaves among the more usual dark-green leaves. **Flowers:** Infrequently, January–April; terminal clusters of 8–10, white pendant cups 10 mm across, 8 mm long. **Fruit:** Blue, ellipsoid, 20 mm long.

Family Epacridaceae

Fitzgeraldii
Dracophyllum fitzgeraldii

Large endemic spreading tree to 13 m high, forming dense canopy. Found from Erskine Valley to summit of mountains. **Leaves:** Alternate, linear, 20 x 1 cm, tapering to point. **Flowers:** December–April; about 100 white tubular flowers 6 mm long in spike to 12 cm. **Fruit:** 2 mm across, brown globular capsule.

Leucopogon parviflorus

Upright shrub to 1.5 m, with long branches and dense foliage. Common on mountain ledges and lowland flats and ridges. **Leaves:** Stiff, 2 x 0.5 cm, widest at top, crowded on terminal branchlets. **Flowers:** July–November; 4 mm long, white with hairs on petals; crowded in short spikes between stem and leaf. **Fruit:** 3 mm in diameter, green, turning translucent yellow when ripe.

Family Escalloniaceae

Corokia carpodetoides

An endemic shrub 2 m high, sometimes growing to a 5 m tree; common on Mt Gower. **Leaves:**

Alternate, finely toothed, narrowly elliptical; 5 x 2 cm; top surface shiny light green, underside yellow-green. **Flowers:** December–January; provides one of LHI's most colourful displays – masses of bright-yellow flowers 8 mm across. **Fruit:** Brown, flat, dry, 3 mm across.

Family Euphorbiaceae

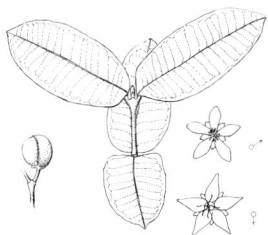

Bloodwood
Baloghia inophylla

Medium tree to 7 m high common on exposed ridges up to 400 m. Common name refers to red sap that oozes from bark when cut. **Leaves:** Opposite, broadly elliptical, stiff and leathery, 7 x 4 cm; abruptly narrowed to short, blunt point. **Flowers:** October–April; small clusters; white, 12 mm across with 4–5 petals. **Fruit:** Hard and globular; green, turning brown when dry, 1.5 cm across.

Greybark
Drypetes deplanchei subsp. *affinis*

Handsome endemic tree to 16 m high; light-grey bark often mottled pink with lichen. Common lowland tree, occasionally found to 500 m. **Leaves:** Alternate, elliptical, 6 x 3 cm, scalloped. **Flowers:** September–January; male flowers green, 6 mm across

with eight stamens; female flowers green and globular, 6 mm across. **Fruit:** Globular, 2 cm across, slightly elongated, bright orange to yellow. Tree very attractive when in fruit.

Dogwood
Omalanthus nutans

Small spreading tree to 5 m high, widespread in moist locations. **Leaves:** Spirally arranged around stem; heart-shaped, 10 x 9 cm on long red stalks. **Flowers:** Spring–summer; on spikes, minute male flowers along shaft, with a few globular females at base. **Fruit:** Globular, compressed, succulent, about 10 mm wide.

Family Fabaceae

Canavalia rosea

Trailing or climbing creeper with stems 2–3 m long, found on beach margins. **Leaves:** Alternate,

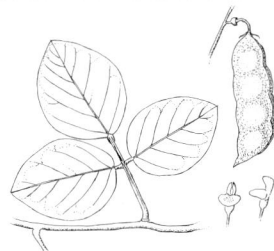

compound, with three 6 x 5 cm leaflets. **Flowers:** Most of year; pink, pea-like, 15 mm long, in clusters of up to 20 on long stalks. **Fruit:** Broad pod 10 x 2 cm, with rib on each side.

Carmichaelia exsul

Endemic broom-like shrub 1–2 m high, found in mountains, usually on exposed rocky ledges above 400 m. **Leaves:** Adult plant leafless or a few compound leaves with three 2 x 1 cm leaflets. **Flowers:** October–December; pea-like, white with purple markings, 7 mm long, in simple branched clusters; faint, sweet perfume. **Fruit:** Thin, flattened pod, 12 mm long.

Mucuna gigantea

Tall woody climber with thick long stems; climbs high into trees. Uncommon and hard to find on LHI; leaves are high up, although

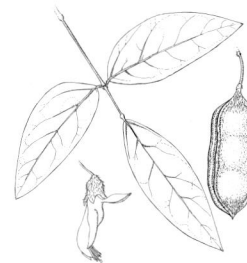

its flowers often fall on walking tracks. **Leaves:** Alternate, compound, three 11 x 5 cm leaflets, dark green. **Flowers:** Mainly October–February; light-green, pea-like, 5 cm long with yellow, irritating hairs; clusters of about 12 hang down like chandeliers. **Fruit:** Broad green capsule 10 cm long with sharp edges and yellow, irritating hairs; never collected on LHI.

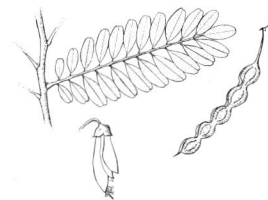

Lignum vitae
Sophora howinsula

Rough-barked endemic tree to 13 m high, scattered throughout lowland hills. Very hard timber has been used for fenceposts and house stumps. **Leaves:** Compound, with up to 11 pairs of elliptical, 20 x 8 mm leaflets. **Flowers:** July–September; large, yellow, pea-like, 3–4 cm long in clusters of several to 20. **Fruit:** A pod 7–12 cm long, green, turning light brown.

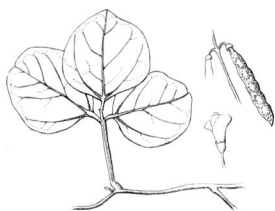

Vigna marina

Trailing or climbing creeper with stems 2–3 m long. Common on dunes and beach margins. **Leaves:** Alternate, compound, three circular leaflets 5 x 4 cm. **Flowers:** Most of year; yellow, pea-like, 15 mm long, in clusters on long stalks. **Fruit:** Narrow pod 8 x 1 cm, sides twisting in spirals as they dry.

Family Flacourtiaceae

Xylosma maidenii

Small endemic tree to 5 m high, common in dry forest areas from sea level to about 300 m. **Leaves:** Alternate, thin, wavy, toothed, 6 x 3 cm; yellow-orange stem. **Flowers:** December–June; minute, green, between stem and leaf or clustered on bare twigs. **Fruit:** Purple, globular, 6 mm across.

Xylosma parvifolium

Rare endemic bush 1–2 m high, found near the top of Mt Gower.

Leaves: Alternate, egg-shaped, 1.2 x 0.8 cm, toothed; red-brown stem. **Flowers:** December–June; 2 mm, green, between stem and leaf. **Fruit:** Purple, globular, 5 mm across.

Family Gesneriaceae

Pumpkin tree
Negria rhabdothamnoides

Handsome endemic tree to 8 m high with white corky bark. Common from 500 m up and occasionally lower (e.g. Erskine Creek at 150 m). **Leaves:** In whorls of three; glossy, egg-shaped, 20 x 10 cm. **Flowers:** October–April; bell-shaped, 27 x 18 mm; orange with small red dots. **Fruit:** Black capsule 15 mm long.

Family Lamiaceae

Westringia viminalis

Compact, endemic shrub less than 0.5 m high, found mainly on mountain ledges and cliffs at 350–450 m. **Leaves:** Crowded, in whorls of four; linear, 15 x 2 mm, underside covered in fine white hairs. **Flowers:** April–December; white, 13–18 mm long, petals in five lobes. **Fruit:** Nutlet, 1.6–2.2 mm long.

Family Lauraceae

Native blackbutt
Cryptocarya gregsonii

Endemic tree to 12 m high, abundant at the Saddle and on Mt Gower's summit. **Leaves:** Alternate, roundish, 8 x 5.5 cm; thick and leathery; top shiny, dark green; underside yellow-green. **Flowers:** November–February; minute, green, in small clusters. **Fruit:** Black, globular, about 4 cm across.

Blackbutt
Cryptocarya triplinervis

Dark-trunked small to medium tree to 16 m high. One of the most common lowland trees, found up to 400 m altitude. **Leaves:** Alternate, 7 x 3 cm with three distinctive veins from the base of the leaf. **Flowers:** November–February; 3 mm across, cream to yellowish, in clusters. **Fruit:** Black, globular, 12 mm long.

Family Loganiaceae

Geniostoma huttonii

Scrambling endemic shrub to 1 m discovered on Mt Lidgbird in 1991. **Leaves:** Opposite, egg-shaped, 2.5 x 1.2 cm. **Flowers:** January–March, pairs or singles between leaf and stem; white, 5 mm long, five petals, odourless. **Fruit:** Round green capsule 6 mm across.

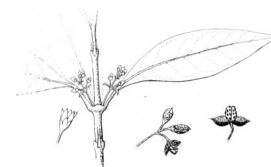

Boar tree
Geniostoma petiolosum

Small endemic 2–4 m tree, found in sheltered forests below 450 m. **Leaves:** Opposite, 11 x 3.5 cm, tapering at both ends. **Flowers:** October–January; white, 8 mm long, in small clusters; emit a pungent odour smelt up to 10 m away. **Fruit:** Round capsule 5 mm across, green drying to black.

Family Malvaceae

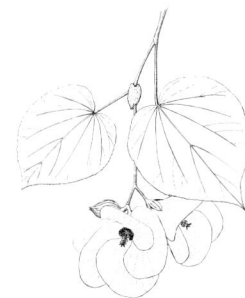

Hibiscus tiliaceus

Spreading tree to 10 m high, rare on LHI. Scattered occurrence on lowlands. Early island residents boiled bark to use as fishing line. **Leaves:** Alternate, heart-shaped, 12 x 12 cm, soft. **Flowers:** November–April; bell-shaped, 8 cm across, pale yellow, turning red on falling. **Fruit:** Five-celled brown capsule with irritating hairs inside; about 25 mm long.

Sallywood
Lagunaria patersonia

Straight-trunked tree to 15 m high, common on lowlands. **Leaves:** Alternate, elliptical, 8 x 3.5 cm; underside covered in dense white scales. **Flowers:** October–February; 5 cm diameter, hibiscus-like, white with pink tinges. **Fruit:** Brown, globular 20 mm round capsule with stiff irritating hairs inside.

Family Meliaceae

Island apple
Dysoxylum pachyphyllum

Common endemic tree growing to 2 m on ridges, 8 m in forest. Found from sea level to summits. **Leaves:** Compound, with up to 12 leaflets on short stalk. **Flowers:** February–August; light-green, tubular, 10 mm long; 20–30 on a 40 cm floral stalk growing from trunk or lower branches. **Fruit:** In clusters along stalk; globular, brown, hard, 4 cm across.

Family Menispermaceae

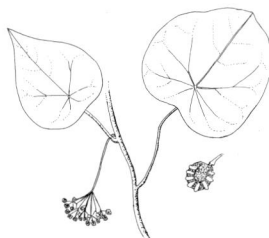

Stephania japonica var. *timoriensis*

Slender uncommon climber found in understorey of moist lowland forests. **Leaves:** Alternate, round, up to 10 cm across; stalk attached to lower surface, not margin. **Flowers:** Summer; minute, in small clusters. **Fruit:** Compressed pulpy fruit, 5 mm across.

Family Moraceae

Banyan
Ficus macrophylla
subsp. *columnaris*

Endemic tree to 20 m high, easily recognised by many thick trunks and dangling roots that eventually form new trunks. Common on lowlands. **Leaves:** Alternate or spiralled around stem, egg-shaped, 16 x 10 cm; yellow underside is noticeable from afar when windblown. **Flowers:** Most of year; many flowers enclosed in hollow globular display ("fig"),

2 cm across. **Fruit:** Purple, 2 cm across, fermenting when fallen.

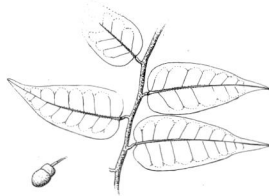

Trophis scandens subsp. *megacarpa*

Endemic, woody climber with rough stem that will cling to a hand rubbed over it; common in lowland forests. **Leaves:** Alternate, 13 x 5 cm, oblong-elliptical, tapering to long point; leathery and stiff. **Flowers:** Spring–summer; males minute, in cylindrical spikes to 10 mm long; females in globular heads 4 mm in diameter. **Fruit:** Bright-red berry, 12 mm across.

Family Myoporaceae

Juniper
Myoporum insulare

Tree to 4 m widespread in lowlands to 300 m, especially in areas exposed to salt air. **Leaves:** Alternate, tapering at both ends, shiny, 6 x 1.5 cm. **Flowers:** Mainly December–June; white, 8 mm in diameter, purple dots on petals. **Fruit:** fleshy, purple, 8 mm across.

Family Myrsinaceae

Mangrove
Aegiceras corniculatum

Mangrove shrub to 3 m found at mouths of lowland creeks flowing into lagoon. **Leaves:** Alternate, egg-shaped, 6 x 2.5 cm, leathery. **Flowers:** September–March; white, 8 mm long, in clusters. **Fruit:** Horn-shaped with a long point; 30 mm long, purple-green.

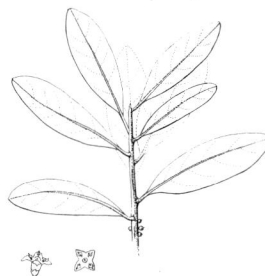

Rapanea mccommishii

Rare endemic tree to 15 m high, ranging from sea level to summits. **Leaves:** Alternate, narrowly elliptical, 5–12 x 1.7–4 cm, conspicuous pale midrib; brown dots seen when held to light. **Flowers:** May–June; minute. **Fruit:** Globular, fleshy, 5 mm across.

Rapanea myrtillina

Rare endemic shrub to 3 m high found mainly on mountain summits, but occasionally down to

400 m. **Leaves:** Alternate, tapering at both ends, 1.1 x 0.4 cm, brown dots on surface. **Flowers:** May–June; minute and cream with dark pink spots; on stems and in clusters. **Fruit:** Purple, globular, 4 mm across.

Rapanea platystigma

An endemic shrub to 3 m, occasionally small tree to 6 m. Widespread on lowlands and ridges to about 400 m. **Leaves:** Dense, alternate, wavy margins sometimes slightly rolled under, 4 x 1.5 cm. **Flowers:** August–September; minute, greenish with red spots; numerous on stems and in clusters. **Fruit:** Globular, 4 mm across, purple when ripe.

Family Myrtaceae

Scalybark
Syzygium fullagarii

Endemic tree to 20 m with massive spreading limbs and red-

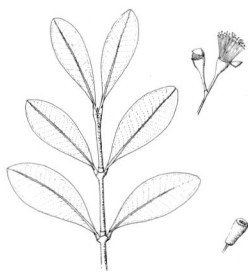

brown bark that comes off in scales. Prominent buttresses. Common in sheltered forests to about 400 m. **Leaves:** Opposite, 9 x 3 cm, shiny. **Flowers:** January–April; cream, 25 mm long in clusters; similar to eucalypt flowers. **Fruit:** Deep red, conical, 20 mm long; most noticeable when it falls on tracks in winter.

Tea-tree
Leptospermum polygalifolium subsp. *howense*

Rough-barked endemic spreading tree to 5 m high, found mainly near mountain tops. **Leaves:** Alternate, elliptical, 8 x 2 mm; conspicuous brown oil dots. **Flowers:** November–January; white, 15 mm across. **Fruit:** Woody, 6 mm in diameter domed capsule with five valves.

Tea-tree
Melaleuca howeana

Endemic low to tall shrub with thin, flaky bark. Common on exposed sites, e.g. cliffs, seashore and ridges. **Leaves:** Alternate, 10 x 2 mm, linear with blunt tips, translucent oil dots. **Flowers:** September–December; pale cream, 5 mm long; about 25 in short spikes on branch ends. **Fruit:** Short, woody capsule, 3 mm across.

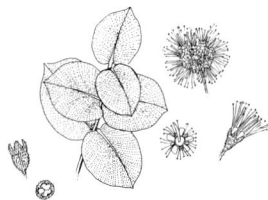

Mountain rose
Metrosideros nervulosa

Stunted endemic shrub 1 m high on exposed ridges, to 8 m high tree in forest. Grows mainly from 400 m to summits. Those in moist sites have roots dangling from branches to take in airborne moisture. **Leaves:** Opposite, stiff, elliptical-round, 3.5 x 3 cm. **Flowers:** October–January; deep red, small petals, densely clustered; numerous stamens to 2 cm long. **Fruit:** Woody capsule, 6–8 mm long.

Mountain rose
Metrosideros sclerocarpa

Small endemic tree to 10 m high found mainly in watercourses around southern mountains, to about 300 m. **Leaves:** Opposite, elliptical to egg-shaped, 5 x 2.5 cm, smooth and glossy. **Flowers:** December–February; bright red, but not as striking as those of *M. nervulosa;* dense clusters. **Fruit:** Woody capsule 6–7 mm across.

Family Nyctaginaceae

Punkwood
Pisonia brunoniana

Shrub or small tree to 4 m. Trunk has prominent white corky spots. A common understorey plant of lowland forest. **Leaves:** Alternate, 16 x 6 cm, elliptical to rhomboid, dark glossy green on top. **Flowers:** July–January; funnel-shaped, 10 x 5 mm, pale green; in upright, branched clusters. **Fruit:** 2–3 cm long, five ribs, black, very sticky.

Family Oleaceae

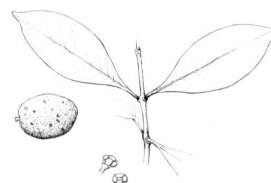

Blue plum
Chionanthus quadristamineus

White-barked endemic tree to 16 m high, common in sheltered forests of southern mountains to 400 m. **Leaves:** Opposite, tapering at both ends, 5–12 x 3–5 cm, shiny dark green on top. **Flowers:** November–April; green, 5 mm across; in clusters. **Fruit:** Egg-shaped, 5–6 cm long, purple; seen on ground most of year.

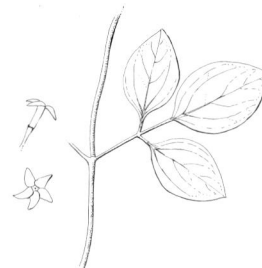

Jasmine
Jasminum didymum subsp. *didymum*

Climber, 3–4 m tall with dense foliage, common on lowlands and ridges to 300 m; climbs bushes and trees. **Leaves:** Opposite, compound; three egg-shaped leaflets, largest about 5 x 3 cm. **Flowers:** February–October; white, star-shaped, 6 x 8 mm; in clusters of up to 50; strong, sweet perfume. **Fruit:** Black, globular, fleshy berry, 10 mm across.

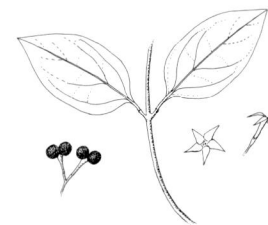

Jasmine
Jasminum simplicifolium subsp. *australiense*

Scrambling shrub or climber, 10 m tall, with dense foliage, climbing into bushes and trees in lowland forests and on ridges. **Leaves:** Opposite, simple, egg-shaped to elliptical, 6 x 3.5 cm, distinct joint in stem. **Flowers:** October–June; white, star-shaped, 8 x 10 mm; in clusters of up to 40; strong, sweet perfume. **Fruit:** Shiny black globular berry, 12 mm across.

Maulwood
Olea paniculata

Widespread 14 m high tree in lowland forest up to 500 m. Small white dots on trunk, branches and roots. **Leaves:** Opposite, egg-shaped to elliptical, pointed, 7 x 3.5 cm, glossy dark green. **Flowers:** August–November; white, minute; numerous in sprays. **Fruit:** Black, curved, 8 mm long.

Family Passifloraceae

Passiflora herbertiana
subsp. *insulae-howei*

Widespread soft-wooded endemic climber. Stems several metres long. **Leaves:** Alternate, simple, up to 11 x 12 cm, with three broad, shallow, triangular lobes. **Flowers:** October–March; orange-yellow to greenish, 6 cm across. **Fruit:** Oval green berry, 4–5 cm long; edible, but sickly sweet.

Family Piperaceae

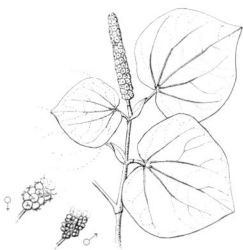

Kava
Macropiper excelsum
subsp. *psittacorum*

Endemic, woody shrub to 1.5 m high; common understorey plant of lowlands. **Leaves:** Alternate, heart-shaped, 6–10 cm across, 5–8 cm long, five major veins. **Flowers:** July–September; minute, no petals; male spikes to 16 cm long, female spikes to 8 cm long. **Fruit:** Small, orange, fleshy berries; top flattened with dimple in centre; sweet when ripe December–January.

Macropiper hooglandii

Woody shrub 2–3 m high; thicker stems than *M. excelsum*; abundant in damp, shaded conditions on mountain slopes. **Leaves:** Alternate, heart-shaped, 8–13 cm across, 7–12 cm long, seven main veins; strongly aromatic and peppery. **Flowers:** September–November; minute, no petals; male on spikes to 10 cm long, female spikes to 6 cm. **Fruit:** Red fleshy berries, 10 mm in diameter; arranged along spikes; hard and pungent; peppery when ripe; March–May.

Family Pittosporaceae

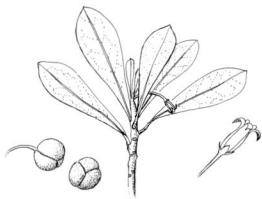

Pittosporum erioloma

Endemic tree to 8 m, common from 450 m to mountain tops. **Leaves:** Alternate, 5 x 1.5 cm, margins rolled over; clustered at ends of branchlets. **Flowers:** Mainly August–October; bell-shaped with petals rolled back, lilac with white tips, 13 mm x 6 mm. **Fruit:** Green, thick-walled capsule 15 mm across.

Family Polygonaceae

Muehlenbeckia complexa

Small shrub forming a dense, semi-prostrate tangled mass with red-brown, thin stems. Grows on open coastal sites, e.g. Blinky Beach dune, or open rocky sites such as Malabar Hill. **Leaves:** Roundish, thick, 9 x 8 mm, bright green. **Flowers:** January–May; small; male has eight stamens, female has a three-lobed stalk. **Fruit:** Small (2 mm long) brown nut.

Family Ranunculaceae

Clematis glycinoides

Soft-wooded low creeper. Reasonably common from sea level to 500 m. **Leaves:** Opposite, compound with three 4–7 x 3–4.5 cm leaflets. **Flowers:** September–November; white, 25 mm across, in clusters. **Fruit:** Tight cluster of 2 mm dry fruits, each with a long, feathery attachment, forming a loose "cotton ball".

Family Rubiaceae

Green plum
Atractocarpus stipularis

Attractive endemic tree growing to about 12 m. Found from sea level to the mountain tops. **Leaves:** Opposite, broad egg-shaped, 20 x 12 cm. **Flowers:** November–February; white, 21 mm across; clusters of up to 20 or so between leaf and stem; strong, pleasant perfume, very noticeable on Boat Harbour track in early summer. **Fruit:** Large green berry 4 cm long; ferments when fallen.

Coprosma huttoniana

Endemic shrub 1–3 m high, common in mountains from 500 m.

Leaves: Opposite, blunt tip, veins come off midrib at angle of about 50°; unpleasant odour when crushed. **Flowers:** May–July; 8 mm long, green; males in clusters, females single or in pairs. **Fruit:** Red, oval, 10 mm long.

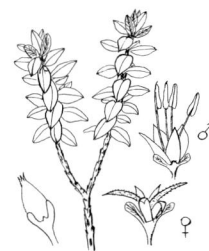

Coprosma inopinata

Rare, compact, scrambling or prostrate shrub to 0.5 m high. Only discovered in 1989 on a ridge off the summit of Mt Gower, also seen on Mt Lidgbird. **Leaves:** Opposite, tapering to a long point, 11 x 6 mm; mid-green above, whitish green below. **Flowers:** October–November; green with purple margins, crowded between leaf and stem; male 9 mm long with 4 mm petals, female 6 mm long with 1 mm petals. **Fruit:** Egg-shaped, fleshy, translucent orange, 6 x 3 mm.

Family Rutaceae

Coprosma lanceolaris

Endemic shrub 1–3 m, common from 500 m. Differentiated from *C. buttoniana* by bright-green fleshy leaves and veins come off mid-rib at an angle of about 30°. **Leaves:** Opposite, long point, 4 x 2 cm, unpleasant odour when crushed. **Flowers:** June–August; green, 5 mm long, female in pairs or single, male in clusters of three. **Fruit:** Egg-shaped, red, 6–8 mm long.

Goatwood
Coprosma prisca

Endemic shrub to 3 m high, found in lowland areas especially near coast, e.g. behind Blinky Beach. **Leaves:** Opposite, oblong-elliptic, 6 x 2.5 cm, margins rolled over, crispy. **Flowers:** September–October; green, 8 mm long; females single or pairs, males in clusters of three. **Fruit:** Green, fleshy 7 mm long.

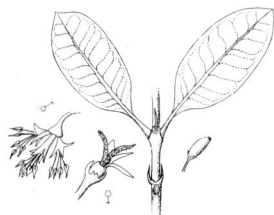

Stinkwood
Coprosma putida

Endemic shrub or small tree to 4 m tree, common in sheltered forests. **Leaves:** Opposite, oblong-elliptical, 7 x 4 cm; putrid odour when bruised or crushed. **Flowers:** August–November; green, 8 mm long; females single or pairs, males in clusters of three. **Fruit:** Red, fleshy, 2 cm long; also has putrid odour.

Black grape
Psychotria carronis

Dark-trunked endemic tree to 8 m high. Uncommon, found mainly at an altitude of 100–400 m in moist forests of southern mountains. **Leaves:** 11 x 4 cm, tapering at both ends, glossy, dark green with white midrib and veins; stem has prominent ring-like leaf scars. **Flowers:** November–March; white, 8 x 6 mm in stalked clusters. **Fruit:** Shiny, black, fleshy; 18–20 mm long; in a loose cluster.

Melicope contermina

Rare endemic shrub; 2 m high in open, to 5 m tree in forest; several plants in Erskine Valley and above first rope on Mt Gower track. **Leaves:** Opposite, compound, with three elliptical leaflets, 9 x 3 cm. **Flowers:** November–January; white, 8 mm long, in clusters. **Fruit:** Capsule with four pointed lobes, each 16 mm long; green turning brown.

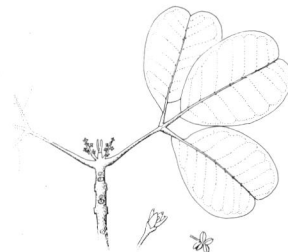

Melicope polybotrya

Endemic tree to 8 m high, reasonably common in sheltered forests to about 500 m. **Leaves:** Opposite, clustered at branchlet ends; compound, with three heart-shaped, 9 x 7 cm leaflets. **Flowers:** December–February; green, 7 mm long, in clusters. **Fruit:** Brown capsule consisting of four segments, each 5–6 mm long.

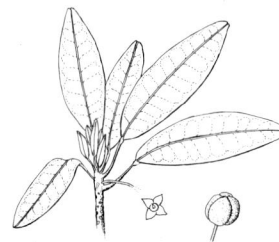

Yellow wood
Sarcomelicope simplicifolia
subsp. *simplicifolia*

Uncommon tree to 6 m high found on all lowland ridges. **Leaves:** Opposite, often in clusters of three, narrowly elliptical, 8 x 3 cm, clustered at branch ends; oil dots on leaf. **Flowers:** June–September; white, 7 mm across, in clusters. **Fruit:** Hard, cream, globular, 12 mm across.

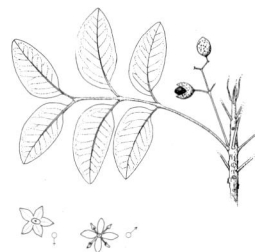

Yellow wood
Zanthoxylum pinnatum

Uncommon tree to 8 m high, found on most lowland ridges. **Leaves:** Opposite, compound, with up to eight egg-shaped 5 x 2.5 cm leaflets crowded at branchlet ends. **Flowers:** April–August; white, 4–5 petals, 7 mm across, in clusters. **Fruit:** Purple capsule, 8 mm across, oily dots on surface; fragrant when cut.

Family Santalaceae

Exocarpus homalocladus

Broom-like endemic shrub to 2 m, or 4 m tree. Found from sea level to mountain tops. **Leaves:** Adult mainly leafless with flattened branchlets; juveniles have linear 6 x 1 cm leaves. **Flowers:** March–July; minute, yellow-green, stalkless; in clusters between stem and leaf. **Fruit:** Red, fleshy, 8 mm long; sits on red swollen stalk that turns translucent pink when fruit is ripe.

Family Sapindaceae

Hopwood
Dodonaea viscosa
subsp. *burmanniana*

Shrub to 2 m or tree to 4 m with fibrous bark and slightly sticky leaves and twigs. Common and widespread in exposed lowland areas. **Leaves:** Alternate, 7 x 1.5 cm, wavy edges, shiny, conspicuous veins. **Flowers:** May–July; no petals, green; males 6 mm long, females 10 mm long. **Fruit:** 15 mm long, three-winged capsule with papery wings, drying purple-brown.

Cedar
Guioa coriacea

Endemic tree to 15 m common in sheltered forest below 500 m. **Leaves:** Alternate, compound with 2–6 leaflets, 7 x 2.5 cm, leaf margins strongly rolled under; shiny. **Flowers:** December–February; white with pink tinges, 6 mm across; in clusters. **Fruit:** Green-brown woody capsules, to 25 mm across; three narrow lobes.

Family Sapotaceae

Axe-handle wood
Pouteria myrsinoides reticulata

Tree to 6 m tall, common on lowlands and ridges. **Leaves:**

Alternate, 7 x 3.5 cm, leathery, slightly shiny. Shoot-tips and young leaves are covered in red hairs. **Flowers:** May–July; green, 8 mm long, inconspicuous; in clusters of 2–6 between leaf and stem. **Fruit:** 13 mm long, narrow egg-shaped berry with a point.

Family Solanaceae

Solanum aviculare

Soft-wooded shrub to 2 m tall. Previously more common, now found mainly in mountain areas. **Leaves:** Alternate, linear, 10 x 2 cm, or deeply lobed. **Flowers:** November–March; purple, 20–30 mm across, in loose clusters. **Fruit:** Orange-red, oval berry, 10–20 mm long.

Family Symplocaceae

Symplocus candelabrum

Endemic tree to 13 m tall with very dark, smooth trunk, found in sheltered forests of southern mountains to about 400 m. **Leaves:** Alternate, tapering to

a long point; 13 x 5 cm, turn yellow when fallen. **Flowers:** April–June; white with yellow tips, 10 mm across; in spikes between leaf and stem. **Fruit:** Bluish, oval-shaped, 12 mm long.

Family Thymelaeaceae

Pimelia congesta

Endemic shrub to 1 m high with tough, red bark. Reasonably common, usually found on dry exposed ridges. **Leaves:** Opposite, in four successive pairs at right angles, linear, 1.8 x 0.3 cm. **Flowers:** July–December; white, 15 mm long, about nine flowers in each head. **Fruit:** Brown, dry, oval nut, 2–3 mm long.

Family Ulmaceae

Cottonwood
Celtis conferta subsp. *amblyphylla*

Endemic tree to 16 m high with whitish bark, common and widespread in lowland forests.

Leaves: Alternate, elliptical, 8 x 3.5 cm; thick and leathery. **Flowers:** November–February; males 4 mm across, in clusters, female spherical, 3 mm diameter. **Fruit:** Purple, globular, 4 mm long.

Family Urticaceae

Boehmeria calophleba

Endemic tree to 3–6 m tall, locally abundant in wet forest areas of southern mountains. **Leaves:** Alternate, egg-shaped, 10 x 3.5 cm, toothed, silver-white underneath, dark green above. **Flowers:** October–April, minute, in clusters along the ends of branches; the stamens spring out to release pollen into the air. **Fruit:** Dry, 4 mm long.

Family Violaceae

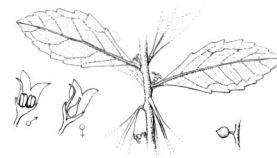

Melicytus novae-zelandieae

Rare endemic shrub to 1 m high, occasionally a small tree to 5 m. Found near Kims Lookout, Goat House Cave and Eddies Cave. **Leaves:** Alternate, elliptical,

6 x 2.5 cm. **Flowers:** August–October; green-yellow, 2 mm across. **Fruit:** Purple berry, 6 mm across.

Family Winteraceae

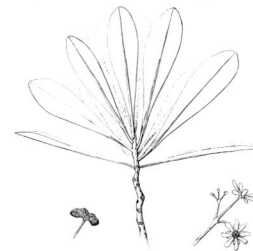

Hot bark
Zygogynum howeanum

Endemic tree to 13 m high with a dark, smooth trunk. Common in sheltered forests from sea level to mountain tops. **Leaves:** Straplike, 18 x 5 cm, shortly tapered to a blunt point, clustered at branch ends. **Flowers:** June–December; white, 20 mm across with 8–10 long thin petals, in small clusters. **Fruit:** Tight cluster of 3–6 black berries, each 10 x 7 mm.

Seabirds

Providence petrel
Pterodroma solandri

Dark pigeon-sized bird. Breeds in winter and only on LHI (apart from a few pairs around Norfolk Island). Nests in short burrows, mainly on higher parts of mountains. **Description:** Length 40 cm, wingspan 94 cm. Dark-grey upper surfaces with paler underparts; cream triangular patches under wings; white scaly feathers around face. Bill stout, black; legs black.

Kermadec petrel
Pterodroma neglecta

Medium-sized dark bird. Breeds on Balls Pyramid in late summer. At sea, tends to be solitary, flying with deep wingbeats followed by long glides, dipping to catch squid and crustaceans. **Description:** Length 38 cm, wingspan 92 cm. Many colour variations, from entirely dark brown with a few flecks of grey

on face and neck, to sooty brown above with pale-grey head and white underparts. LHI Kermadecs are mainly dark. White bases to primary flight feathers flash white on upper and lower wing surfaces. Bill short, black; legs, feet flesh-coloured.

Black-winged petrel
Pterodroma nigripennis

Small grey-and-white petrel with loud, high-pitched calls. Seen in spirited summer courtship flights over its burrows along the cliffs

at Neds Beach, Transit Hill and Mutton Bird Pt. **Description:** Length 30 cm, wingspan 65 cm. Upper body pale grey, underparts white; crown dark, face white, spotted with black; black patch around each eye; upper wings and tail slate grey; underwing white with broad black margins. Bill black; legs, feet flesh-coloured.

Flesh-footed shearwater or muttonbird
Puffinus carneipes

Largest and most common of the shearwaters breeding at LHI. Colonies at Neds Beach, Middle Beach and The Clear Place. Congregates in large rafts just offshore before flying in at dusk. Makes a raucous wailing at night. **Description:** Length 46 cm, wingspan 102 cm. Uniform dark brown to black. Bill heavy, straw-coloured, dark tip; feet flesh-coloured.

Wedge-tailed shearwater
Puffinus pacificus

Nesting in burrows on offshore islands (including Blackburn) and on Mutton Bird Pt, Signal Pt, Lovers Bay and in north hills, this bird makes a soft wailing sound. **Description:** Length 43 cm, wingspan 100 cm. Entirely sooty brown; tail long, wedge-shaped. Bill slender, slate-grey; feet flesh-coloured.

Little shearwater
Puffinus assimilis

Small black-and-white shearwater, recognised in flight by its short glides followed by rapid wingbeats. A winter breeder, it nests in burrows, mainly on

offshore islands. **Description:** Length 28 cm, wingspan 62 cm. Upper surfaces bluish black, underparts chalky white; underwings white with narrow black margins. Bill short, slender, blue-grey and black; feet blue, webs flesh.

White-bellied storm-petrel
Fregetta grallaria

Compact storm-petrel with a square-cut tail. Nests on offshore islands in crevices and cavities among loose stones. Often seen at sea pattering the water with its feet as it feeds on plankton. **Description:** Length 20 cm, wingspan 40 cm. Upper parts, head and throat black; rump and underparts white; underwing variable – mostly white with black leading edge. Bill, legs, feet black.

Masked booby or gannet
Sula dactylatra fullagari

Large, non-migratory bird often seen flying along the coast alone or in small parties. Breeds on offshore islands and at Mutton Bird and King points, the species' southernmost breeding locations. Builds a rough nest of flattened grass. **Description:** Length 87 cm, wingspan 170 cm. White overall with black tips to tail and flight

Birds

feathers and a black mask around eyes and bill. Bill yellow; legs, feet grey. Immatures have brown head, tail and flights.

Red-tailed tropicbird or bosun bird
Phaethon rubricauda

Large, majestic white bird well known for aerobatic displays. Summer breeder, with colonies along cliffs of northern hills and around southern mountains. **Description:** Length 46 cm, and two stiff, red tail streamers to 50 cm, wingspan 105 cm. All white with pink flush to feathers; black patches around eyes. Bill red; legs pale blue, feet black.

Sooty tern or wideawake
Sterna fuscata

The most numerous of seabirds nesting at LHI, this distinctive bird has colonies on all offshore islands as well as Mt Eliza and

Neds Beach, laying one speckled egg on the ground. **Description:** Length 46 cm, wingspan 90 cm. Head and upper parts black; underparts and forehead white. Tail deeply forked. Bill, feet black.

Common or brown noddy
Anous stolidus

Grey-brown tern commonly seen flying slowly along cliffs near its colonies in north hills, offshore islands, Blinky Beach and Mutton Bird Pt. **Description:** Length 40 cm, wingspan 82 cm. Uniform black-brown body and wings; lighter grey crown and white forehead. Tail wedge-shaped with central notch. Beak and legs black.

Black noddy
Anous minutus

Darker and slightly smaller than the common noddy, this long-billed bird is often seen flying just

offshore, particularly around cliffs of northern hills. Small breeding colony at North Bay. **Description:** Length 36 cm, wingspan 70 cm. Sooty black all over; distinct white forehead and crown. Slightly forked tail. Bill black, slender; feet black.

White tern
Gygis alba

A favourite among islanders and visitors; breeding location along Lagoon Road allows close observation of this beautiful white bird. Balances one egg in depression on low branch and rears chick there. **Description:** Length 30 cm, wingspan 75 cm. Body white all over with long wings and a forked tail. Large brown eyes finely ringed in black. Bill blue-black; legs black.

Grey ternlet or blue billie
Procelsterna cerulea

Long-legged, light-grey ternlet remains at LHI all year; seen on cliffs around offshore islets and north hills. **Description:** Length 28 cm, wingspan 52 cm. Body and wings pale blue-grey; paler face and breast; large eyes ringed with black at front, white behind. Bill slender, black; feet black, yellow webs.

Land birds

Pacific black duck and hybrid mallard
Anas superciliosa and *A. superciliosa x A. platyrhynchos*

Seen around golf course and – unusually – in salt water at Neds Beach. **Description:** Length 58 cm. Hybrids have colour variations. Body mottled brown with cream tips to feathers. Wing-patch green or blue, barred with black and white at each end.

Male mallards have glossy green head, white collar and purplish brown breast; underside white with fine black lines; white tail.

White-faced heron
Ardea novaehollandiae

Large blue-grey bird with long S-shaped neck, often seen foraging in grassy areas, and along rocky seashore and beaches at low tide. Builds large, rough nest of sticks high in trees. **Description:** Length 67 cm. Blue-grey with darker flight feathers. Face and throat white. Beak black; legs and feet olive-yellow.

Australian or nankeen kestrel
Falco cenchroides

Large-winged brown falcon often seen 10 m above open paddocks or cliffs, hovering motionless in search for mice, grasshoppers and beetles. Small population on LHI. **Description:** Length 32 cm. Upper parts rufous brown with fine black spotting on back; face and underparts white, rump and tail grey with black bar near white tip. Female has brown

rump and tail. Beak blue-grey; legs yellow.

Buff-banded rail
Gallirallus philippensis

Small rail with beautiful patterns of brown, black and white on feathers. Inhabits wet paddocks, the golf course and more recently, settled areas. **Description:** Length 30 cm. Upper parts olive-brown, mottled black and white; crown olive-brown; face grey with chestnut band through eye to neck; chin white, throat grey; underparts barred black and white with a broad chestnut band across the breast. Beak flesh-brown; legs, feet brown.

Woodhen
Tricholimnas sylvestris

One of the world's rarest birds, this endemic flightless rail is very territorial, responding to noise by calling and running to warn off intruders. Feeds on worms and other soil invertebrates by scratching leaf litter with its beak. Nest of grass, moss and small twigs in petrel burrows or hollows under tree roots. **Description:** Length 36 cm. Body olive-brown all over; reduced flight feathers are barred chestnut and black. Bill pinkish grey, 50 mm, slightly downward-curved; legs, feet grey.

Purple or eastern swamphen
Porphyrio porphyrio

Omnivorous black-and-blue long-legged rail with red bill. Seen around golf course, airstrip and Cobbys Corner. Nests in thick long grass, particularly near swampy areas. **Description:** Length 48 cm. Upper parts and face dusky black; breast, belly deep blue; underbelly black, white under tail. Beak and forehead shield bright red; legs pink.

Masked lapwing
Vanellus miles

Medium-sized bird, usually seen in groups of 4–6 feeding in pastures on insects, spiders, larvae and worms. Very distinctive staccato alarm call to warn chicks of approaching intruders. **Description:** Length 36 cm. Upper parts grey-brown, underparts white; crown to sides of breast black; rump and tail white; face white with yellow wattles. Black-tipped yellow spur on each shoulder. Beak pale yellow; legs red.

Emerald dove or ground-dove
Chalcophaps indica

Very tame brown-and-green pigeon; most commonly seen land bird on LHI. A solitary bird of open lowland forest, where it's often heard cooing softly. Builds rough platform nest of twigs 1–3 m off ground. **Description:** Length 24 cm. Bright-green wings and shoulders with white elbow patches; general body red-brown with back crossed by two grey bands. Beak orange with red base; legs and feet red-brown. Female has smaller, grey elbow patches and dull back bands.

Masked owl
Tyto novaehollandiae

Large nocturnal bird of prey; hides in tree hollows during day. About 80 released on LHI in 1920s in unsuccessful attempt to control rats. **Description:** Length 40 cm (male) to 50 cm (female). Upper parts blackish-brown speckled with white; underparts white to pale buff spotted black. Face cream to fawn. Beak white; legs covered with dense white down; feet off-white with long claws.

Sacred kingfisher
Todiramphus sanctus

Striking, long-billed, blue-green bird often seen sitting patiently on fences. Nests in tree hollows. **Description:** Length 20 cm. Wings, tail, rump bright blue; back dull-green; head green with black band from bill around nape and buff spot in front of eye.

Underparts buff to white. Bill black; feet and legs grey to black.

Magpie-lark
Grallina cyanoleuca

Familiar ground-feeder seen all over lowlands in cleared areas and in sparsely timbered forest margins. Builds a solid nest of mud, twigs and palm fibre on high branches. **Description:** Length 28 cm. Upper parts black with several broad patches of white; underparts white. Male has black throat and face; female has white throat and forehead. Beak off-white; legs black.

Lord Howe pied currawong
Strepera graculina crissalis

Large, black bird with strong melodious call. Often encountered while on forest tracks in island's southern parts, where it shows great interest in visitors. Larger beak and smaller white patches than mainland currawong. **Description:** Length 46 cm.

Plumage sooty black with small patches of white on wing, rump and tail. Eye yellow; beak large, black; feet, legs black.

Welcome swallow
Hirundo neoxena

Small bird usually seen in small groups sitting on fences or flying fast and low over paddocks or swamps, catching insects on the wing. Makes mud nest in humans' structures or seashore caves. **Description:** Length 15 cm. Upper parts shiny blue-black; underparts whitish-fawn; throat and forehead rufous; tail deeply forked, dusky with white bars below. Beak, legs black.

Lord Howe Island white-eye or silvereye
Zosterops tephropleura

Smallest and most numerous of LHI's endemic land birds, ranging all over island. Often seen in groups flitting through trees; suspends its small cup-shaped nest from branches. **Description:** Length 13 cm. Upper parts generally yellow-green; back and sides grey, belly white. Head and throat yellow with white eye ring. Beak brown; legs grey-brown.

Common blackbird
Turdus merula

Most common bird of settled area. Male has strong and melodious song, or loud "tchink tchink" alarm call. Nests around and under houses. **Description:** Length 25 cm. Male all black with yellow eye ring; beak orange; feet black. Female dark brown with grey chin and brown bill and feet.

Song thrush
Turdus philomelos

Light-brown bird mainly found in lowland forest and settlement area. Male produces melodic song of repeated phrases in spring and summer, especially at dawn and dusk. **Description:** Length 23 cm. Upper parts olive-brown; throat pale yellow, speckled brown; breast buff with small triangular patches; belly white. Beak brown; legs pink.

Lord Howe golden whistler or yellow robin
Pachycephala pectoralis contempta

Small bird commonly seen in lowland forests, hopping from branch to branch seeking insects. Some very tame, entering households or lodges for food. **Description:** Length 17 cm. Male has black head, white throat with broad black band below; shoulders, breast and belly bright yellow; upper body olive-grey, wings dusky with yellow tinge; tail, beak and legs black. Female has olive-grey upper parts; underparts grey with yellowish wash; belly buff, throat speckled whitish.

Common starling
Sturnus vulgaris

Dark, stocky bird with short tail, upright stance and jaunty walk. Feeds mostly on open grassy areas of airstrip and golf course. Perhaps only 30 on island today. **Description:** Length 21 cm. Black all over with green/purple sheen except for brown wash on wings and tail. Fresh plumage is often speckled brown, which gradually changes to black. Beak brown (yellow when breeding); legs brown.

Regular visitors

Cattle egret
Ardea ibis

Small white heron regularly seen in grassy paddocks, where it forages for insects disturbed by cattle. Small numbers seen at LHI in May–June and November–December. A few winter on island. **Description:** Length 50 cm. Body all white with yellow-green skin around face. Beak pale yellow; feet olive-yellow. In November–December breeding plumage of feathers around crown, neck and back tinged with orange-buff; facial skin reddish; beak red with yellow tip.

Bar-tailed godwit
Limosa lapponica

Large bird, mottled grey and brown, seen during summer in groups of 4–8 on grassy areas, especially around airport and golf course. **Description:** Length 40 cm. Upper parts mottled grey and brown; lower back, rump and tail barred with white and brown; underparts white with some grey on breast. Beak 8 cm long with pink base and black tip; legs and feet grey. Breeding plumage: head, neck and underparts rich rufous colour.

Whimbrel
Numenius phaeopus

Usually seen during summer, alone in remote, wetter paddocks or marine weed flats at low tide. Loud melodious trill if disturbed. **Description:** Length 41 cm. Mainly buff with upper parts mottled dark and light brown. Crown brown with grey median

stripe and white eyebrow strips. Throat and breast streaked with brown. Beak 9 cm long, brown and down-curved. Legs and feet grey.

Ruddy turnstone
Arenaria interpres

During summer frequents beaches and open grassy areas in flocks of up to 20. Runs quickly from one feeding patch to another. When approached will quickly fly off, making its white underparts very noticeable. **Description:** Length 23 cm. Upper parts brown mottled with grey, black and white. Underparts white with broad dark-brown patch on each side of breast. Beak black; legs and feet orange. Breeding plumage: upper part black and chestnut, head white, crown grey, upper breast black.

Pacific golden plover
Pluvialis fulva

Summer visitor, usually feeding alone or in small groups in grassy paddocks or along seashores. **Description:** Length 24 cm. Upper parts mottled brown with golden flecks; breast mottled grey-brown and buff; abdomen white; underwings white-grey. Bill black; legs slate-grey.

Double-banded plover
Charadrius bicinctus

Visiting March–August, this small grey-and-white plover is usually seen alone around airstrip or on beaches. **Description:** Length 18 cm. Upper parts grey-brown; forehead and eyebrows white; underparts off-white. As winter progresses it develops breeding plumage with two broad bands on chest, black upper and red-brown lower. Beak black; legs, feet grey-green.

Further Reading

Clark, H. 'The Paradise of the Tasman'. *National Geographic*, vol. LXVIII, July 1935.

Cogger, H. 'The Reptiles of Lord Howe Island'. *Proceedings of the Linnean Society of NSW*, no. 91, 1971.

Coupe, R. *Australia's Wilderness Heritage*, vols 1 and 2. Weldon, Sydney, 1988.

Doubilet, D. 'Lord Howe Island: Australian Haven in a Distant Sea'. *National Geographic*, vol. 180, no. 4, October 1991.

Edgecombe, J. *Lord Howe Island World Heritage Area*. Australasian Environmental Publications, 1987.

Finch, A. and V. Finch. *Lord Howe Island*. Rigby, Adelaide, 1967.

Gaffney, E. 'The Cranial Morphology of the Extinct Horned Turtle *Meiolania Platyceps*, from Lord Howe Island, Australia'. *Bulletin of the American Museum of Natural History*, vol. 175. New York, 1983.

Gillett, K. and F. McNeil. *The Great Barrier Reef and Adjacent Islets*. Coral Press, Sydney, 1959.

Green, P. *Flora of Australia vol. 49: Oceanic Islands 1.* AGPS, Canberra, 1994.

Hill, C. 'Lord Howe Island'. *Australian Geographic*, no. 28, Oct/Dec 1992.

Hindwood, K. 'The Birds of Lord Howe Island'. *Emu*, vol. 40, 1–86, 1940.

Hutton, I. *Discovering Australia's World Heritage: Lord Howe Island*. Conservation Press, Canberra, 1986.

Hutton, I. *Ramblers Guide to Lord Howe Island*. Hutton, Coffs Harbour, 1990.

Hutton, I. *Birds of Lord Howe Island: Past and Present*. Hutton, Coffs Harbour, 1991.

Hutton, I. 'Coral Graveyards of the Pacific – Middleton & Elizabeth Reefs'. *GEO*, vol. 14, no. 3, October 1992.

Hutton, I. 'Changing Birdlife of an Island'. *Birds International*, vol. 3, no. 1, 1991.

Lord Howe Island Board, Regional Environmental Study, vols. 1–10. Lord Howe Island Board, Sydney, 1985.

McDougall, I., B. Embleton and D. Stone. 'Origin and Evolution of Lord Howe Island: SW Pacific Ocean'. *Journal of the Geological Society of Australia*, vol. 28, no. 2, 1981.

Rabone, H. *Lord Howe Island: Its Discovery and Early Associations 1788–1888*. Australis Publications, Sydney, 1940.

McFadyen, K. *Pinetrees: Lord Howe Island 1842–1992*. Pinetrees, Lord Howe Island, 1992.

Nicholls, M. *A History of Lord Howe Island*. Mercury Walsh, Tasmania, 1975.

Pickard, J. 'Vegetation of Lord Howe Island'. *Cunninghamia*, vol. 2, 1983. Royal Botanic Gardens, Sydney.

Recher, H. and S. Clarke. *Environmental Survey of Lord Howe Island*. NSW Govt Printer, Sydney, 1974.

Rodd, A. *XIII International Botanical Congress Field Trip 17: Lord Howe Island*. Australian Academy of Sciences, Canberra, 1981.

Veron, J. and T. Done. 'Corals and Coral Communities of Lord Howe Island'. *Australian Journal of Marine and Freshwater Research*, vol. 30, no. 2, 1979.

Wilson, J. Bowie. *Lord Howe Island: A Report on the Present State and Future Prospects*. NSW Govt Printer, 1882; facsimile, NSW Govt Printer, Sydney, 1981.

Index

Index